Windows Debugging

Practical Foundations

Dmitry Vostokov

OpenTask

Published by OpenTask, Republic of Ireland

OpenTask books are available through booksellers and distributors worldwide. For further information or comments send requests to:

press@opentask.com

A CIP catalogue record for this book is available from the British Library.

ISBN-13: 978-1-906717-10-0 (Paperback)

First printing, 2009

Revision 1.1

Summary of Contents

Contents

To Debuggers

Preface

This book grew partially from original lectures I developed almost 5 years ago to train support and escalation engineers in debugging and crash dump analysis of memory dumps from Windows applications, services and systems. At that time, when thinking about what material to deliver, I realized that solid understanding of fundamentals like pointers is needed to analyze stack traces beyond !analyze -v and lmv WinDbg commands. Therefore this book is not about bugs or debugging techniques but about background knowledge everyone needs to start experimenting with WinDbg and learn from practical experience and read other advanced debugging books. This body of knowledge is what the author of this book possessed before starting memory dump analysis using WinDbg 5 years ago which resulted recently in the number one debugging bestseller: multi-volume Memory Dump Analysis Anthology. Now, in retrospection, I see these practical foundations as relevant and necessary to acquire for beginners as they were 5 years ago because operating systems internals, assembly language and compiler architecture haven't changed in 5 years and majority of Windows systems are still 32-bit today or applications are executed in 32-bit compatibility mode on x64 Windows systems. For someone, who wants to learn these foundations in the context of 64-bit environments the author is developing a separate x64 supplement and plans to publish it a few months later after this publication is released (ISBN: 978-1-906717-56-8).

When writing this book I realized that more practical examples were needed and I recompiled every sample with the recent Visual C++ Express Edition and provided detailed steps for WinDbg usage. I also recreated almost every illustration to fit and look better in the book format.

The book is useful for:

- Software technical support and escalation engineers
- Software engineers coming from managed code or Java background
- Software testers
- Engineers coming from non-Wintel environments
- Windows C/C++ software engineers without assembly language background
- Security researchers without assembly language background
- Beginners learning Windows software reverse engineering techniques

This book can also be used as Intel assembly language and Windows debugging supplement for relevant undergraduate level courses.

If you encounter any error please contact me using this form

http://www.dumpanalysis.org/contact

or send me a personal message using this contact e-mail:

dmitry.vostokov@dumpanalysis.org

Acknowledgements

The idea of the lecture course title "Practical Foundations of Debugging" and this book subtitle "Practical Foundations" came to me when I started reading Paul Taylor's book "Practical Foundations of Mathematics". Mario Hewardt and Daniel Pravat's book "Advanced Windows Debugging" suggested me the book title "Windows Debugging".

Cover design was done with the help of Aleksey Golikov who found the real bug, shown on this book front cover, in the woods of Udmurtia, Russia, and my wife Ekaterina, who helped me to make a few pictures of it. My son Kirill, one of the youngest book authors on this planet (he is the coauthor of the book "The Lion Meets the Fox") was patient during the last 3 weeks of writing after I explained him the importance of 0's and 1's by reading and playing with "Baby Turing" book I coauthored previously with my daughter Alexandra and published in 2008.

I would like to thank all engineers suggested me to write a book after attending my lectures and debugging seminars.

I'm indebted to Narasimha Vedala for his review of draft chapters with numerous suggestions and for finding bugs in my writing.

About the Author

Before October 14, 2003

Dmitry Vostokov is a software development consultant with over 15 years of experience in software engineering. Dmitry has been involved in over 40 software development projects in variety of industries. He had jointly designed and implemented software quality tools used by many companies worldwide. Dmitry was an architect of enterprise document publishing applications for Boeing Commercial Airplanes Group. He started his professional career as a designer and developer of the first pioneer Windows applications for voice recognition, verification and speech synthesis.

On October 14, 2003

Dmitry joined Citrix as an Escalation Development Analysis Engineer and later became EMEA Development Analysis Team Lead before moving into management. His current position is Technical Manager Dev Analysis EMEA and he lives and works in Dublin, Ireland. He is the author of more than 10 books including the number one debugging book bestseller: multi-volume Memory Dump Analysis Anthology.

Voracious reader, Dmitry maintains several blogs:

Crash Dump Analysis and Debugging
http://www.DumpAnalysis.org/blog

Management Bits and Tips
http://www.ManagementBits.com

Literate Scientist
http://www.LiterateScientist.com

Software Generalist
http://www.SoftwareGeneralist.com

SoftwareAstrology
http://www.SoftwareAstrology.com

Chapter 1: Memory, Registers and Simple Arithmetic

Memory and Registers inside an Idealized Computer

Computer memory consists of a sequence of memory cells and each cell has a unique address (location). Every cell contains a "number". We refer to these "numbers" as contents at addresses (locations). Memory access is slower than arithmetic instructions and to improve this there are so called registers to speed up complex operations that require memory to store temporary results. We can also think about them as standalone memory cells. The name of a register is its address.

Address (Location): 100	0
Address (Location): 101	0
Address (Location): 102	1
Address (Location): 104	1
Address (Location): 105	2
Address (Location): 106	0

Register 1

0

Register 2

10

Picture 1.1

Memory and Registers inside Intel 32-bit PC

Here addresses for memory locations containing integer values usually differ by 4 and we also show 2 registers called EAX and EDX.

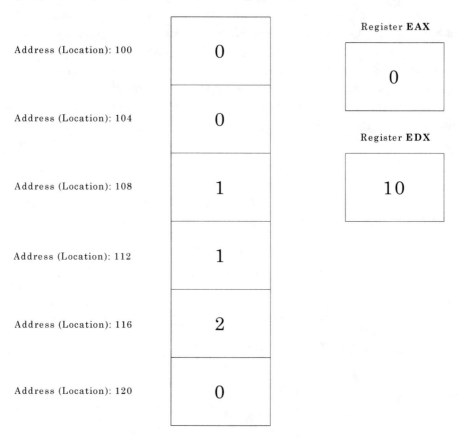

Picture 1.2

Because memory cells contain "numbers" we start with simple arithmetic and ask a PC to compute a sum of two numbers to see how memory and registers change their values. We call our project "Arithmetic".

"Arithmetic" Project: Memory Layout and Registers

For our project we have two memory addresses (locations) that we call "a" and "b". We can think about "a" and "b" as names of their respective addresses (locations). Now we introduce a special notation where [a] means contents at the memory address (location) "a". If we use C or C++ language to write our project then we declare and define memory locations "a" and "b" as:

```
static int a, b;
```

By default, when we load a program, static memory locations are filled with zeroes and we can depict our initial memory layout after loading the program as shown on Picture 1.3.

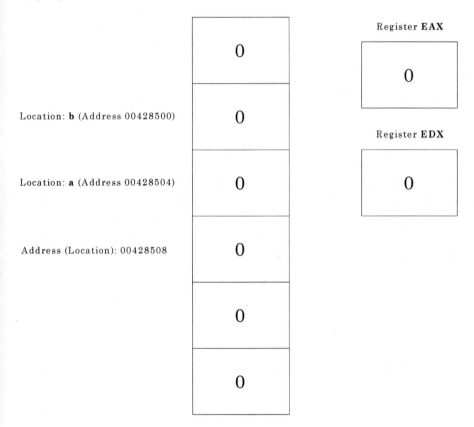

Picture 1.3

"Arithmetic" Project: A Computer Program

We can think of a computer program as a sequence of instructions for manipulation of contents of memory cells and registers. For example, addition operation: add the contents of memory cell №12 to the contents of memory cell №14. In our pseudo-code we can write:

```
[14] := [14] + [12]
```

Our first program in pseudo-code is shown on the left of the table:

`[a] := 1`
 	
`[b] := 1`
 	
`[b] := [b] + [a]   ; [b] = 2`
 	
`[b] := [b] * 2     ; [b] = 4`
	Here we put assembly instructions corresponding to pseudo code.

':=' means assignment when we replace the contents of a memory location (address) with the new value. ';' is a comment sign and the rest of the line is comment. '=' shows the current value at a memory location (address).

To remind, a code written in a high-level programming language is translated to a machine language by a compiler. However, the machine language can be readable if its digital codes are represented in some mnemonic system called assembly language. For example, **INC [a]**, increment by one what is stored at a memory location **a.**

"Arithmetic" Project: Assigning Numbers to Memory Locations

We remind that "a" means location (address) of the memory cell, and it is also the name of location (address) 00428504 (see Picture 1.3). [a] means the contents (number) stored at the address "a".

If we use C or C++ language "a" is called "variable a" and we write assignment as:

```
a = 1;
```

In Intel assembly language we write:

```
mov [a], 1
```

In WinDbg disassembly output we see the following code where the variable "a" is prefixed by '!' and the name of the executable file (module) which is ArithmeticProject.exe:

```
mov dword ptr [ArithmeticProject!a (00428504)], 1
```

We show the translation of our pseudo code into assembly language in the right column:

[a] := 1	mov [a], 1
[b] := 1	mov [b], 1
[b] := [b] + [a] ; [b] = 2	
[b] := [b] * 2 ; [b] = 4	

After the execution of the first two assembly language instructions we have the memory layout shown on Picture 1.4.

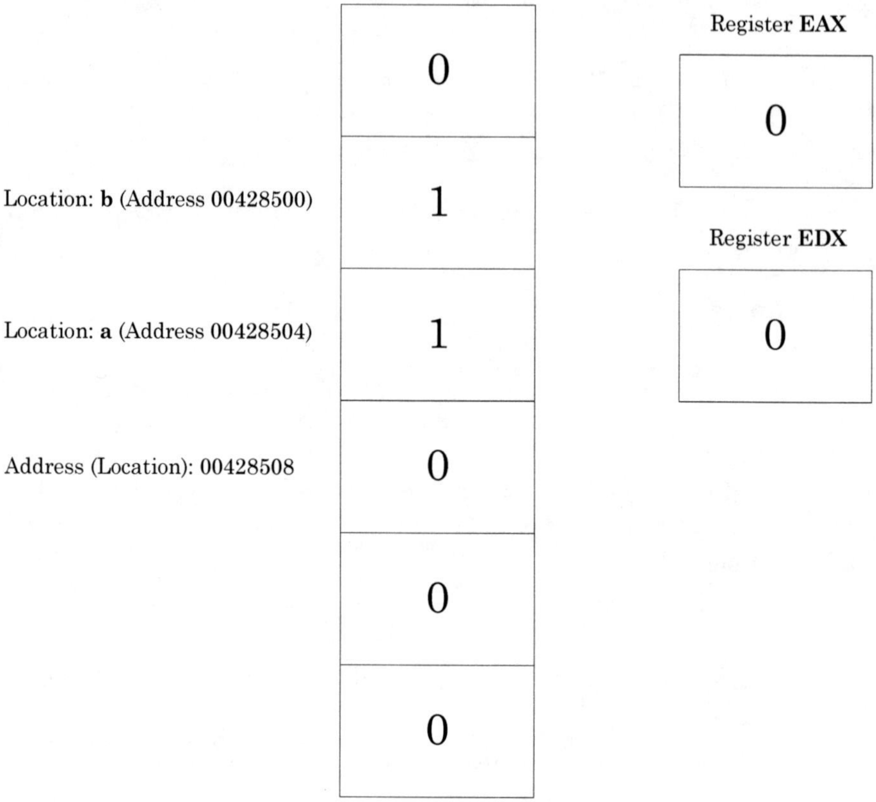

Register **EAX**

0

Location: **b** (Address 00428500)

0

1

Register **EDX**

Location: **a** (Address 00428504)

0

1

Address (Location): 00428508

0

0

0

Picture 1.4

Assigning Numbers to Registers

This is similar to memory assignments. We can write in pseudo-code

```
register := 1 or register := [a]
```

Note that we do not use brackets when refer to register contents. The latter instruction means assigning (copying) the number at the location (address) "a" to a register.

In assembly language we write:

```
mov eax, 1

mov eax, [a]
```

In WinDbg disassembly output we see the following code:

```
mov eax, [ArithmeticProject!a (00428504)]
```

"Arithmetic" Project: Adding Numbers to Memory Cells

Now let's look at the following pseudo-code statement in more detail:

```
[b] := [b] + [a]
```

To recall, "a" and "b" mean the names of locations (addresses) 00428504 and 00428500 respectively (see Picture 1.4). [a] and [b] mean contents at addresses "a" and "b" respectively, simply some numbers stored there.

In C or C++ language we write the following statement:

```
b = b + a; // or

b += a;
```

In assembly language we use instruction ADD. Due to limitations of Intel x86 architecture we cannot use both memory addresses in one step (instruction), for example **add [b], [a]**. We can only use **add [b], register** to add the value stored in **register** to the contents of memory cell **b.** Recall that **register** is like a temporary memory cell itself here:

```
register := [a]

[b] := [b] + register
```

In assembly language we write:

```
mov eax, [a]

add [b], eax
```

In WinDbg disassembly output we see the following code:

```
mov eax,[ArithmeticProject!a (00428504)]

add [ArithmeticProject!b (00428500)],eax
```

Now we can translate our pseudo code into assembly language:

`[a] := 1`	`mov [a], 1`
`[b] := 1`	`mov [b], 1`
`[b] := [b] + [a] ; [b] = 2`	**`mov eax, [a]`**
`; eax = 1`	**`add [b], eax`**
`[b] := [b] * 2 ; [b] = 4`	

After the execution of ADD instruction we have the memory layout illustrated on Picture 1.5.

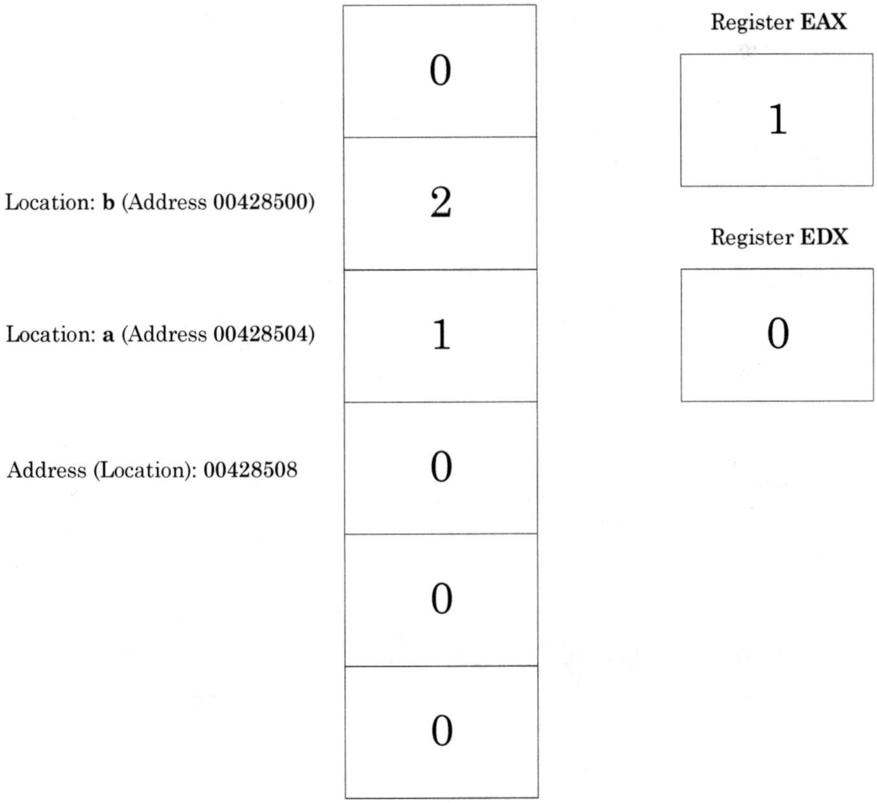

0
Location: b (Address 00428500)
2
Location: a (Address 00428504)
1
Address (Location): 00428508
0
0
0
Register EAX
1
Register EDX
0

Picture 1.5

Incrementing/Decrementing Numbers in Memory and Registers

In pseudo-code it looks simple and means increment (decrement) a number stored at location (address) "a":

```
[a] := [a] + 1

[a] := [a] - 1
```

In C or C++ language we can write this using three possible ways:

```
a = a + 1; // or

++a; // or

a++;

b = b - 1; // or

--b; // or

b--;
```

In assembly language we use instructions INC and DEC and write:

```
inc     [a]

inc     eax

dec     [a]

dec     eax
```

In WinDbg disassembly output we see the same instruction:

```
inc     eax
```

Now we add this additional increment to our pseudo-code and its assembly language translation (this is needed for subsequent multiplication, which is explained later):

[a] := 1	```mov [a], 1```
[b] := 1	```mov [b], 1```
[b] := [b] + [a] ; [b] = 2	```mov eax, [a]```
; eax = 1	```add [b], eax```
eax := eax + 1 ; eax = 2	**```inc eax```**
[b] := [b] * 2 ; [b] = 4	

After the execution of INC instruction we have the memory layout illustrated on Picture 1.6.

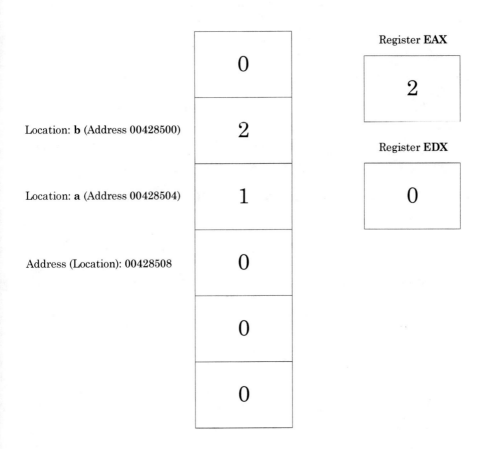

Picture 1.6

Multiplying Numbers

In pseudo code we write:

```
[b] := [b] * 2
```

This means that we multiply the number at the location (address) "b" by 2.

In C or C++ language we can write this using two ways:

```
b =  b * 2; // or

b *= 2;
```

In assembly language we use instruction IMUL (Integer MULtiply) and write:

```
imul [b]

mov  [b], eax
```

The whole sequence means [b] := [b] * eax, so we have to put 2 into eax (see previous section). Fortunately we already have 2 in eax register. The result of multiplication is put into registers eax and edx (for reasons why we need the second register see the next section).

In WinDbg disassembly output we see the following code:

```
imul    dword ptr [ArithmeticProject!b (00428500)]

mov     [ArithmeticProject!b (00428500)],eax
```

Now we add two additional assembly instructions to our pseudo-code assembly language translation:

[a] := 1	`mov    [a], 1`
[b] := 1	`mov    [b], 1`
[b] := [b] + [a] ; [b] = 2	`mov  eax, [a]`
; eax = 1	`add  [b], eax`
eax := eax + 1 ; eax = 2	`inc  eax`
[b] := [b] * 2 ; eax = 4	**`imul [b]`**
; [b] = 4	**`mov  [b], eax`**

After the execution of **imul** and **mov** instructions we have the memory layout illustrated on Picture 1.7.

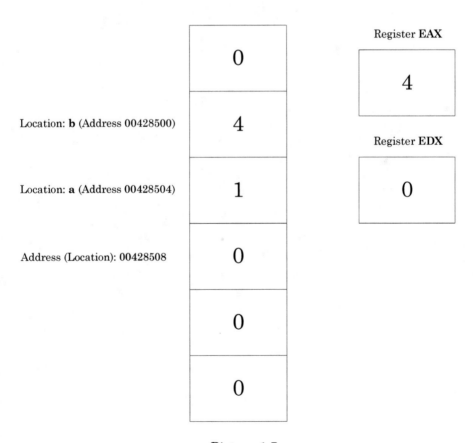

Picture 1.7

Multiplication and Registers

Why do we need two registers to store the result of a multiplication? This is because each register or integer memory cell on x86 PC can contain a number between -2147483648 and 2147483647. If we multiply 2 by 2 the result can be put into one register eax. However, if we multiply 2147483647 by 2147483647 we get 4611686014132420609. The result is too big to fit into one register or memory cell.

We can think of EDX:EAX pair as two memory cells joined together to hold the large multiplication result.

Chapter 2: Debug and Release Binaries

"Arithmetic" Project: C/C++ Program

Let's rewrite our "Arithmetic" program in C++. Corresponding assembly language instructions are put in comments:

```
int a, b;
int main(int argc, char* argv[])
{
        a = 1;          // mov [a], 1
        b = 1;          // mov [b], 1
        b = b + a;      // mov eax, [a]
                        // add [b], eax
        ++a;            // inc eax
                        // mov [a], eax
        b = a * b;      // imul [b]
                        // mov [b], eax
        // results: [a] = 2 and [b] = 4
        return 0;
}
```

If we compile and link the program in debug mode we get the binary executable module which we can load in WinDbg and inspect assembly code.

Downloading and Configuring WinDbg Debugger

WinDbg from Debugging Tools for Windows can be downloaded from Microsoft web site or we can use windbg.org pointing to a Microsoft download link as shown on Picture 2.1.

Picture 2.1

For 64-bit version of Windows we need to download 64-bit Debugging Tools and use WinDbg 64-bit even for debugging 32-bit applications. This book uses 64-bit WinDbg for the first and 32-bit WinDbg for all subsequent exercises. After downloading and installing Debugging Tools we start WinDbg as shown on Picture 2.2.

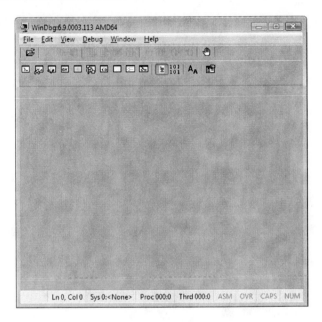

Picture 2.2

WinDbg Disassembly Output – Debug Executable

The Debug executable can be downloaded from the following location:

ftp://dumpanalysis.org/pub/WDPF/Chapter2/

It is located under ArithmeticProjectC\Debug subfolder. First we run WinDbg as an Administrator (requires elevation on Windows Vista) and then load ArithmeticProjectC.exe (menu File\Open Executable...) as shown on Picture 2.3.

Picture 2.3

We see a command line window at the bottom where we can enter WinDbg commands. The first command we enter is to specify a download folder for symbol files needed to interpret OS binary data as shown on Picture 2.4. These files will be downloaded from Microsoft internet symbol server on demand when needed. This command is also featured on windbg.org page as was shown on Picture 2.1.

Picture 2.4

We also need symbol files for our project to interpret binary data in our own executable file. Fortunately this symbol file which has .PDB file extension is located in the same folder where .EXE resides and we don't need a command to specify its path here.

Next we put a **breakpoint** at our **main** C++ function as shown on Picture 2.5 to allow the program execution to stop at that point and give us a chance to inspect memory and registers. Symbolic names/function names like "main" can be used instead of memory locations of the code when symbol file is loaded into WinDbg. This is one useful aspect of a symbol file: we can refer to a function name instead of identifying where the function code resides in the memory.

Picture 2.5

Then we start execution of the program (let it **go**) as shown on Picture 2.6.

Picture 2.6

The program then stops at the previously set breakpoint as shown on Picture 2.7.

Picture 2.7

Now we **u**nassemble main **f**unction as shown on Picture 2.8 and 2.9.

Picture 2.8

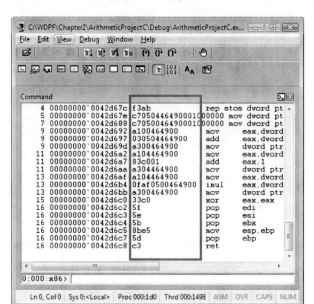

Picture 2.9

The middle column shows binary code we are not interested in and we opt for not including it in the future as shown on Picture 2.10.

Picture 2.10

We repeat our disassembly command as shown on Picture 2.11.

Picture 2.11

We repeat the part of formatted disassembly output here which corresponds to our C++ code where we removed source code line numbers and left only the first 8 digits of memory addresses, for example, 0042d67e is the same as 00000000`0042d67e:

```
0042d67e mov      dword ptr [ArithmeticProjectC!a (00494604)],1

0042d688 mov      dword ptr [ArithmeticProjectC!b (00494600)],1

0042d692 mov      eax,dword ptr [ArithmeticProjectC!b (00494600)]

0042d697 add      eax,dword ptr [ArithmeticProjectC!a (00494604)]

0042d69d mov      dword ptr [ArithmeticProjectC!b (00494600)],eax

0042d6a2 mov      eax,dword ptr [ArithmeticProjectC!a (00494604)]

0042d6a7 add      eax,1

0042d6aa mov      dword ptr [ArithmeticProjectC!a (00494604)],eax

0042d6af mov      eax,dword ptr [ArithmeticProjectC!a (00494604)]

0042d6b4 imul     eax,dword ptr [ArithmeticProjectC!b (00494600)]

0042d6bb mov      dword ptr [ArithmeticProjectC!b (00494600)],eax
```

We can directly translate it to bare assembly code we used in the previous chapter and put corresponding pseudo-code in comments:

```
mov [a], 1     ; [a] := 1
mov [b], 1     ; [b] := 1
mov eax, [b]   ; [b] := [b] + [a]
add eax, [a]   ;
mov [b], eax   ;
add eax, 1     ; [a] := [a] + 1
mov [a], eax   ;
mov eax, [a]   ; [b] := [b] * [a]
imul eax, [b]  ;
mov [b], eax   ;
```

WinDbg Disassembly Output – Release Executable

If we repeat the same procedure for an executable located under ArithmeticProjectC\Release subfolder we get the following output:

```
ArithmeticProjectC!main:
00401000 mov      dword ptr [ArithmeticProjectC!a (0040acc4)],2
0040100a mov      dword ptr [ArithmeticProjectC!b (0040acc0)],4
```

This corresponds to the following pseudo-code:

```
mov [a], 2    ; [a] := 2
mov [b], 4    ; [b] := 4
```

What happened to all our assembly code in this Release executable? If we observe, this code seems to be directly placing the end result into [b]. Why is this happening? The answer lies in a compiler optimization. When the code is compiled in Release mode Visual C++ compiler is able to calculate the final result from the simple C source code itself and generate code only necessary to update corresponding memory locations.

Chapter 3: Number Representations

Numbers and Their Representations

Imagine a herder in ancient times trying to count his sheep. He has a certain number of stones (twelve):

However he can only count up to three and arranges the total into groups of three:

The last picture is a representation (a kind of notation) of the number of stones. We have one group of three groups of three stones plus a separate group of three stones. If he could count up to ten we would see the different representation of the same number of stones. We would have one group of ten stones and another group of two stones.

Decimal Representation (Base Ten)

Let's now see how twelve stones are represented in arithmetic notation if we can count up to ten. We have one group of ten numbers plus two:

$12_{dec} = 1 * 10 + 2$ or $1 * 10^1 + 2 * 10^0$

Here is another exercise with one hundred and twenty three stones. We have **1** group of ten by ten stones, another group of **2** groups of ten stones and the last group of **3** stones:

$123_{dec} = 1 * 10*10 + 2 * 10 + 3$ or $1 * 10^2 + 2 * 10^1 + 3 * 10^0$

We can formalize it in the following summation notation:

$N_{dec} = a_n*10^n + a_{n-1}*10^{n-1} + ... + a_2*10^2 + a_1*10^1 + a_0*10^0$ $0 <= a_i <= 9$

Using the summation symbol we have this formula:

$$N_{dec} = \sum_{i=0}^{n} a_i*10^i$$

Ternary Representation (Base Three)

Now we come back to our herder's example of twelve stones. We have 1 group of three by three stones, 1 group of tree stones and an empty (0) group (which is not empty if we have one stone only of have thirteen stones instead of twelve). We can write down the number of groups sequentially: **110**. Therefore 110 is a ternary representation (notation) of twelve stones and it is equivalent to 12 written in decimal notation:

$$12_{dec} = 1*3^2 + 1*3^1 + 0*3^0$$

$$N_{dec} = a_n*3^n + a_{n-1}*3^{n-1} + ... + a_2*3^2 + a_1*3^1 + a_0*3^0 \qquad a_i = 0 \text{ or } 1 \text{ or } 2$$

$$N_{dec} = \sum_{i=0}^{n} a_i*3^i$$

Binary Representation (Base Two)

In the case of counting up to 2 we have more groups for twelve stones: **1100**. Therefore 1100 is a binary representation (notation) for 12 in decimal notation:

$$12_{dec} = 1*2^3 + 1*2^2 + 0*2^1 + 0*2^0$$

$$123_{dec} = 1*2^6 + 1*2^5 + 1*2^4 + 1*2^3 + 0*2^2 + 1*2^1 + 1*2^0 \text{ or } 1111011_2$$

$$N_{dec} = a_n*2^n + a_{n-1}*2^{n-1} + ... + a_2*2^2 + a_1*2^1 + a_0*2^0 \qquad a_i = 0 \text{ or } 1$$

$$N_{dec} = \sum_{i=0}^{n} a_i*2^i$$

Hexadecimal Representation (Base Sixteen)

If we can count up to sixteen twelve stones fit in one group but we need more symbols: A, B, C, D, E and F for ten, eleven, twelve, thirteen, fourteen and fifteen respectively:

12_{dec} = C in hexadecimal representation (notation)

$123_{dec} = 7B_{hex}$

$123_{dec} = 7*16^1 + 11*16^0$

$$N_{dec} = \sum_{i=0}^{n} a_i * 16^i$$

Why Hexadecimals are used?

Consider this number written in binary notation: 110001010011_2. Its equivalent in decimal notation is 3155:

$$3155_{dec} = 1*2^{11} + 1*2^{10} + 0*2^9 + 0*2^8 + 0*2^7 + 1*2^6 + 0*2^5 + 1*2^4 + 0*2^3 + 0*2^2 + 1*2^1 + 1*2^0$$

Now we divide the binary number digits into groups of four and write them down in decimal and hexadecimal notation:

1100_0101_0011

12$_{dec}$ **5**$_{dec}$ **3**$_{dec}$

C$_{hex}$ **5**$_{hex}$ **3**$_{hex}$

We see that hexadecimal notation is more compact because every four binary digit group number corresponds to one hexadecimal number. Table 3.1 lists hexadecimal equivalents for every four binary digit combination.

In WinDbg and other debuggers memory addresses are displayed in hexadecimal notation.

Binary	Decimal	Hexadecimal
0000	0	0
0001	1	1
0010	2	2
0011	3	3
0100	4	4
0101	5	5
0110	6	6
0111	7	7
1000	8	8
1001	9	9
1010	10	A
1011	11	B
1100	12	C
1101	13	D
1110	14	E
1111	15	F

Table 3.1

Chapter 4: Pointers

A Definition

The concept of a pointer is one of the most important to understand thoroughly to master Windows debugging. By definition, a pointer is a memory cell or a processor register that contains the address of another memory cell as shown on Picture 4.1. It has its own address as any memory cell. Sometimes a pointer is called an indirect address (vs. direct address, the address of a memory cell). Iteratively we can define another level of indirection and introduce a pointer to a pointer as a memory cell or a processor register that contains the address of another memory cell that contains the address of another memory cell and so on.

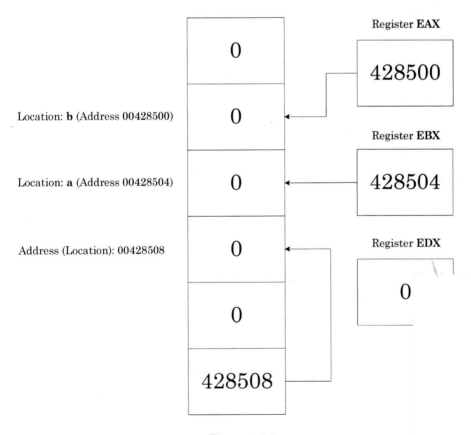

Picture 4.1

"Pointers" Project: Memory Layout and Registers

In our debugging project we have two memory addresses (locations), "a" and "b". We can think about "a" and "b" as names of addresses (locations). We remind that notation [a] means contents at the memory address (location) "a".

We also have registers EAX and EBX *as* pointers to "a" and "b". These registers contain addresses of "a" and "b" respectively. Notation [EAX] means contents of a memory cell whose address is in register EAX.

In C and C++ languages we declare and define pointers to "a" and "b" as:

int *a, *b;

Our project memory layout before program execution is shown on Picture 4.2.

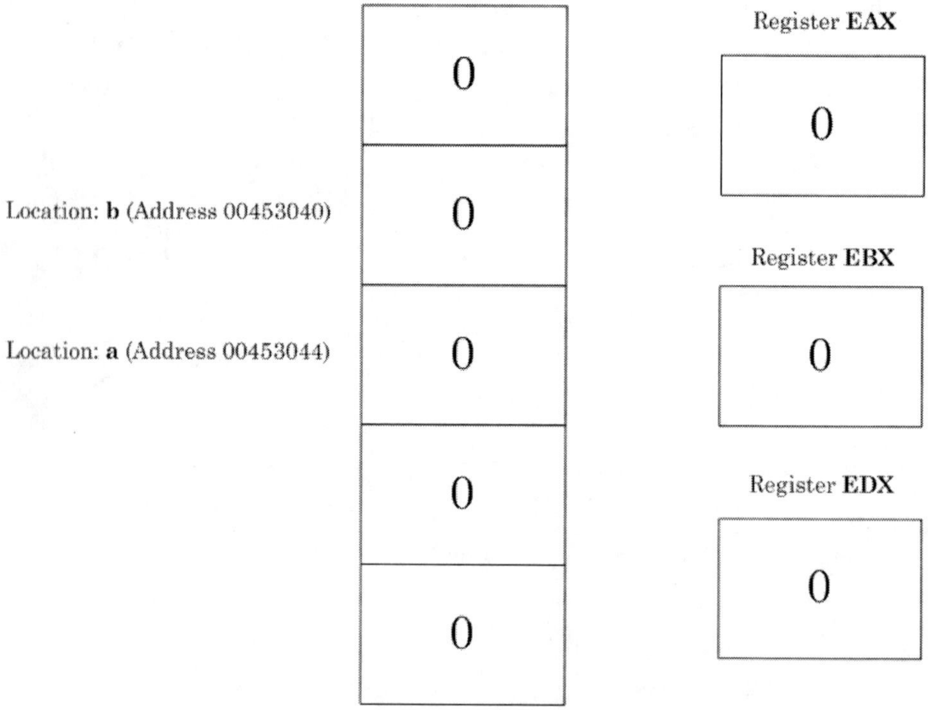

Register **EAX**

Location: **b** (Address 00453040)

Register **EBX**

Location: **a** (Address 00453044)

Register **EDX**

0 0 0 0 0

0 0 0

Picture 4.2

"Pointers" Project: Calculations

In order to understand pointers better from low level assembly language perspective we perform our old arithmetic calculations from Chapter 1 using pointers to memory instead of direct memory addresses:

```
eax := address a

[eax] := 1        ; [a] = 1

ebx := address b

[ebx] := 1        ; [b] = 1

[ebx] := [ebx] + [eax]

                  ; [b] = 2

[ebx] := [ebx] * 2

                  ; [b] = 4
```

Using Pointers to Assign Numbers to Memory Cells

First, the following sequence of pseudo-code instructions means that we use interpret contents of EAX register as the address of a memory cell and then assign a value to that memory cell:

```
eax := address a

[eax] := 1
```

In C language it is called "dereferencing a pointer" and we write:

```
int *a;   // declaration and definition of a pointer

*a = 1;   // get a memory cell (dereference

          // a pointer) and assign a value to it
```

In assembly language we write:

```
lea   eax, a    ; load the address a into eax

mov   [eax], 1  ; use eax as a pointer
```

In WinDbg disassembly output we would see something like this:

```
0040101e 8d0544304500 lea eax, [PointersProject!a (00453044)]

00401024 c60001        mov byte ptr [eax],1
```

The project for this chapter can be downloaded from

ftp://dumpanalysis.org/pub/WDPF/Chapter4/

The executable is located under PointersProject\Debug subfolder. We can load it into WinDbg and disassemble its main function as described in Chapter 2. From now on we will not see screenshots of WinDbg windows but the output from command window instead.

First we load PointersProject.exe using File\Open Executable... menu option in WinDbg and get the following output:

```
CommandLine: "C:\WDPF\PointersProject\Debug\PointersProject.exe"
Symbol search path is: *** Invalid ***
*************************************************************************
* Symbol loading may be unreliable without a symbol search path.        *
* Use .symfix to have the debugger choose a symbol path.                *
* After setting your symbol path,                                       *
* use .reload to refresh symbol locations.                              *
*************************************************************************
Executable search path is:
ModLoad: 00400000 00456000   PointersProject.exe
ModLoad: 7c900000 7c9b0000   ntdll.dll
ModLoad: 7c800000 7c8f4000   C:\WINDOWS\system32\kernel32.dll
(4d8.1b4): Break instruction exception - code 80000003 (first chance)
eax=00251eb4 ebx=7ffd6000 ecx=00000000 edx=00000001 esi=00251f48
edi=00251eb4
eip=7c901230 esp=0012fb20 ebp=0012fc94 iopl=0         nv up ei pl nz na po nc
cs=001b  ss=0023  ds=0023  es=0023  fs=003b  gs=000            efl=00000202
*** ERROR: Symbol file could not be found.  Defaulted to export symbols
for ntdll.dll -
ntdll!DbgBreakPoint:
7c901230 cc               int     3
```

We notice that Symbol search path is invalid and correct this by specifying a location where to put the required symbol files from Microsoft internet symbol server:

```
0:000> .symfix c:\mss
```

Then we put a breakpoint to main function and run the program until WinDbg breaks in:

```
0:000> bp main

0:000> g
Breakpoint 0 hit
eax=00333068 ebx=7ffd6000 ecx=00000001 edx=00333108 esi=01b841d0
edi=01c8f558
eip=00401000 esp=0012ff70 ebp=0012ffb8 iopl=0         nv up ei pl zr na pe nc
cs=001b  ss=0023  ds=0023  es=0023  fs=003b  gs=000            efl=00000246
PointersProject!main:
00401000 55               push    ebp
```

For visual clarity we disable the output of binary codes before disassembling main function:

```
0:000> .asm no_code_bytes
Assembly options: no_code_bytes


0:000> uf main
PointersProject!main [c:\pointersproject\pointersproject.cpp @ 4]:
    4 00401000 push     ebp
    4 00401001 mov      ebp,esp
    4 00401003 sub      esp,0C0h
    4 00401009 push     ebx
    4 0040100a push     esi
    4 0040100b push     edi
    4 0040100c lea      edi,[ebp-0C0h]
    4 00401012 mov      ecx,30h
    4 00401017 mov      eax,0CCCCCCCCh
    4 0040101c rep      stos dword ptr es:[edi]
    7 0040101e lea      eax,[PointersProject!a (00453044)]
    8 00401024 mov      byte ptr [eax],1
   10 00401027 lea      ebx,[PointersProject!b (00453040)]
   11 0040102d mov      byte ptr [ebx],1
   13 00401030 mov      eax,dword ptr [eax]
   14 00401032 add      dword ptr [ebx],eax
   16 00401034 inc      eax
   18 00401035 imul     byte ptr [ebx]
   19 00401037 mov      dword ptr [ebx],eax
   22 00401039 xor      eax,eax
   23 0040103b pop      edi
   23 0040103c pop      esi
   23 0040103d pop      ebx
   23 0040103e add      esp,0C0h
   23 00401044 cmp      ebp,esp
   23 00401046 call     PointersProject!_RTC_CheckEsp (00401050)
   23 0040104b mov      esp,ebp
   23 0040104d pop      ebp
   23 0040104e ret
```

Because we remember that assigning addresses to registers is most likely done by a LEA (Load Effective Address) instruction we put a breakpoint on the address of the first such instruction in the code of main function and then resume the program:

```
0:000> bp 0040101e


0:000> g
Breakpoint 1 hit
eax=cccccccc ebx=7ffd6000 ecx=00000000 edx=00333108 esi=01b841d0
edi=0012ff6c
eip=0040101e esp=0012fea0 ebp=0012ff6c iopl=0      nv up ei pl nz na pe nc
cs=001b  ss=0023  ds=0023  es=0023  fs=003b  gs=0000          efl=00000206
PointersProject!main+0x1e:
0040101e lea     eax,[PointersProject!a (00453044)]
```

Now we examine variables a and b to verify memory layout shown previously on Picture 4.2 using **dc** WinDbg command:

```
0:000> dc PointersProject!a l1
00453044  00000000                            ....


0:000> dc PointersProject!b l1
00453040  00000000                            ....
```

We also clear values of EAX, EBX and EDX registers in accordance to Picture 2:

```
0:000> r eax = 0


0:000> r ebx = 0


0:000> r edx = 0
```

We can verify registers by using **r** WinDbg command:

```
0:000> r
eax=00000000 ebx=00000000 ecx=00000000 edx=00000000 esi=01b841d0
edi=0012ff6c
eip=0040101e esp=0012fea0 ebp=0012ff6c iopl=0      nv up ei pl nz na pe nc
cs=001b  ss=0023  ds=0023  es=0023  fs=003b  gs=0000          efl=00000206
PointersProject!main+0x1e:
0040101e lea     eax,[PointersProject!a (00453044)]
```

Now we execute the first for instructions that correspond to our pseudo-code using **t** WinDbg command (the output of **t** command also shows the instruction to be executed next):

eax := address a	lea eax, a
[eax] := 1 ; [a] = 1	mov eax, 1
ebx := address b	lea ebx, b
[ebx] := 1 ; [b] = 1	mov ebx, 1
[ebx] := [ebx] + [eax]	
; [b] = 2	
[ebx] := [ebx] * 2	
; [b] = 4	

```
0:000> t
eax=00453044 ebx=00000000 ecx=00000000 edx=00000000 esi=01b841d0
edi=0012ff6c
eip=00401024 esp=0012fea0 ebp=0012ff6c iopl=0       nv up ei pl nz na pe nc
cs=001b  ss=0023  ds=0023  es=0023  fs=003b  gs=0000           efl=00000206
PointersProject!main+0x24:
00401024 mov     byte ptr [eax],1                     ds:0023:00453044=00

0:000> t
eax=00453044 ebx=00000000 ecx=00000000 edx=00000000 esi=01b841d0
edi=0012ff6c
eip=00401027 esp=0012fea0 ebp=0012ff6c iopl=0       nv up ei pl nz na pe nc
cs=001b  ss=0023  ds=0023  es=0023  fs=003b  gs=0000           efl=00000206
PointersProject!main+0x27:
00401027 lea     ebx,[PointersProject!b (00453040)]
```

```
0:000> t
eax=00453044 ebx=00453040 ecx=00000000 edx=00000000 esi=01b841d0
edi=0012ff6c
eip=0040102d esp=0012fea0 ebp=0012ff6c iopl=0         nv up ei pl nz na pe nc
cs=001b  ss=0023  ds=0023  es=0023  fs=003b  gs=000              efl=00000206
PointersProject!main+0x2d:
0040102d mov     byte ptr [ebx],1                  ds:0023:00453040=00


0:000> t
eax=00453044 ebx=00453040 ecx=00000000 edx=00000000 esi=01b841d0
edi=0012ff6c
eip=00401030 esp=0012fea0 ebp=0012ff6c iopl=0         nv up ei pl nz na pe nc
cs=001b  ss=0023  ds=0023  es=0023  fs=003b  gs=0000             efl=00000206
PointersProject!main+0x30:
00401030 mov     eax,dword ptr [eax]         ds:0023:00453044=00000001
```

We also see that values of a and b has changed as expected:

```
0:000> dc PointersProject!a l1
00453044  00000001                        ....


0:000> dc PointersProject!b l1
00453040  00000001                        ....
```

All this corresponds to a memory layout shown on Picture 4.3.

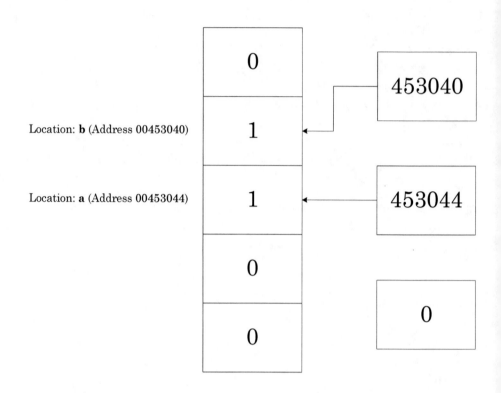

Picture 4.3

Adding Numbers Using Pointers

Now we look at the next pseudo-code statement:

```
[ebx] := [ebx] + [eax]
```

Recall that [eax] and [ebx] mean contents of memory cells whose addresses (locations) are stored in EAX and EBX CPU registers. The statement above is equivalent to the following C or C++ language expression where '*' operator means to get memory contents pointed to by pa or pb pointer (also called pointer dereference):

```
*pb = *pb + *pa;
```

In assembly language we use instruction ADD for '+' operator but we cannot use both memory addresses in one step instruction:

```
add [ebx], [eax]
```

We can only use one memory reference and therefore we need to employ another register as a temporary variable:

```
register := [eax]
[ebx] := [ebx] + register
```

In assembly language we write this sequence of instructions:

```
mov eax, [eax]
add [ebx], eax
```

In WinDbg disassembly output we see these instructions indeed:

```
00401030 mov      eax,dword ptr [eax]
00401032 add      dword ptr [ebx],eax
```

We add them to our pseudo-code table:

eax := address a	lea eax, a
[eax] := 1 ; [a] = 1	mov eax, 1
ebx := address b	lea ebx, b
[ebx] := 1 ; [b] = 1	mov ebx, 1
[ebx] := [ebx] + [eax]	mov eax, [eax]
; [b] = 2	add [ebx],eax
[ebx] := [ebx] * 2	
; [b] = 4	

Now we execute these two instructions (we remind that the output of
t command shows the next instruction to be executed when we use **t** command again):

```
[From previous output]
eax=00453044 ebx=00453040 ecx=00000000 edx=00000000 esi=01b841d0
edi=0012ff6c
eip=00401030 esp=0012fea0 ebp=0012ff6c iopl=0         nv up ei pl nz na pe nc
cs=001b  ss=0023  ds=0023   es=0023   fs=003b   gs=0000            efl=00000206
PointersProject!main+0x30:
00401030 mov      eax,dword ptr [eax]          ds:0023:00453044=00000001


0:000> t
eax=00000001 ebx=00453040 ecx=00000000 edx=00000000 esi=01b841d0
edi=0012ff6c
eip=00401032 esp=0012fea0 ebp=0012ff6c iopl=0         nv up ei pl nz na pe nc
cs=001b  ss=0023  ds=0023   es=0023   fs=003b   gs=0000            efl=00000206
PointersProject!main+0x32:
00401032 add      dword ptr [ebx],eax          ds:0023:00453040=00000001
```

```
0:000> t
eax=00000001 ebx=00453040 ecx=00000000 edx=00000000 esi=01b841d0
edi=0012ff6c
eip=00401034 esp=0012fea0 ebp=0012ff6c iopl=0       nv up ei pl nz na po nc
cs=001b  ss=0023  ds=0023  es=0023  fs=003b  gs=0000           efl=00000202
PointersProject!main+0x34:
00401034 inc     eax
```

We also check the memory location of b variable to see that it really changed its value:

```
0:000> dc PointersProject!b 11
00453040  00000002                              ....
```

All this corresponds to a memory layout shown on Picture 4.4.

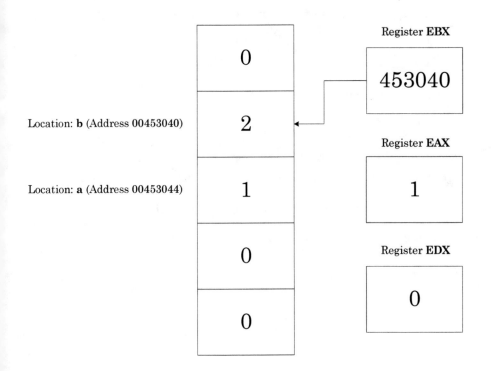

Picture 4.4

Multiplying Numbers Using Pointers

Our next pseudo-code statement does multiplication:

```
[ebx] := [ebx] * 2
```

This statement means that we multiply contents of the memory whose address is stored in EBX register by 2. In C or C++ language we write similar expression as the addition statement we have seen in the previous section (note that we have two distinct meanings of '*' operator, pointer dereference and multiplication):

```
*pb = *pb * 2; // or
```

```
*pb *= 2;
```

The latter is a shorthand notation. In assembly language we use instruction IMUL (Integer MULtiply)

```
imul [ebx]
```

This instruction is equivalent to the following pseudo-code:

```
eax := [ebx] * eax
```

Therefore, we have to put 2 into EAX register, but we already have 1 in EAX so we use INC EAX instruction before IMUL to increment EAX by 1.

In WinDbg disassembly output we would see this:

```
00401034        inc       eax
00401035        imul      byte ptr [ebx]
00401037        mov       dword ptr [ebx],eax
```

We add them to our pseudo-code table:

eax := address a	lea eax, a
[eax] := 1 ; [a] = 1	mov eax, 1
ebx := address b	lea ebx, b
[ebx] := 1 ; [b] = 1	mov ebx, 1
[ebx] := [ebx] + [eax]	mov eax, [eax]
; [b] = 2	add [ebx],eax
[ebx] := [ebx] * 2	inc eax
; [b] = 4	imul [ebx]
	mov [ebx],eax

Now we execute these three instructions (we remind that the output of **t** command shows the next instruction to be executed when we use **t** command again):

[From previous output]
```
eax=00000001 ebx=00453040 ecx=00000000 edx=00000000 esi=01b841d0
edi=0012ff6c
eip=00401034 esp=0012fea0 ebp=0012ff6c iopl=0         nv up ei pl nz na po nc
cs=001b  ss=0023  ds=0023  es=0023  fs=003b  gs=0000            efl=00000202
PointersProject!main+0x34:
00401034 inc     eax
```

```
0:000> t
eax=00000002 ebx=00453040 ecx=00000000 edx=00000000 esi=01b841d0
edi=0012ff6c
eip=00401035 esp=0012fea0 ebp=0012ff6c iopl=0         nv up ei pl nz na po nc
cs=001b  ss=0023  ds=0023  es=0023  fs=003b  gs=0000            efl=00000202
PointersProject!main+0x35:
00401035 imul    byte ptr [ebx]                       ds:0023:00453040=02
```

```
0:000> t
```

eax=00000004 ebx=00453040 ecx=00000000 edx=00000000 esi=01b841d0
edi=0012ff6c
eip=00401037 esp=0012fea0 ebp=0012ff6c iopl=0   nv up ei pl nz na po nc
cs=001b ss=0023 ds=0023 es=0023 fs=003b gs=0000   efl=00000202
PointersProject!main+0x37:
00401037 mov   dword ptr [ebx],eax   ds:0023:00453040=00000002

```
0:000> t
```
eax=00000004 ebx=00453040 ecx=00000000 edx=00000000 esi=01b841d0
edi=0012ff6c
eip=00401039 esp=0012fea0 ebp=0012ff6c iopl=0   nv up ei pl nz na po nc
cs=001b ss=0023 ds=0023 es=0023 fs=003b gs=0000   efl=00000202
PointersProject!main+0x39:
00401039 xor   eax,eax

We check again the memory location of b variable to see that it really changed its value:

```
0:000> dc PointersProject!b l1
00453040   00000004                                   ....
```

All this corresponds to a memory layout shown on Picture 4.5.

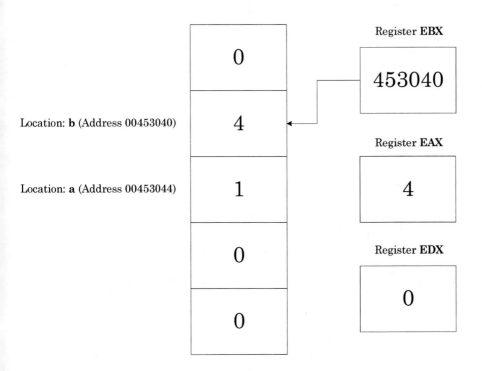

Picture 4.5

Chapter 5: Bytes, Words and Double Words

Using Hexadecimal Numbers

If we want to use hexadecimal number in C language we prefix them with **0x**, for example:

```
a = 12;      // 12_dec

a = 0xC;     // C_hex
```

In WinDbg disassembly output and when entering commands numbers are interpreted as hexadecimal by default although we can still prefix them with **0x**. If we want a number to be interpreted as decimal we prefix it with **0n**, for example:

mov [a], **0n**12

mov [a], C

mov [a], 0xC

Byte Granularity

Picture 5.1 shows the difference between bytes, words and double words in terms of byte granularity. We see that each successive size is double of the previous. There are also quad words with the size of 8 bytes.

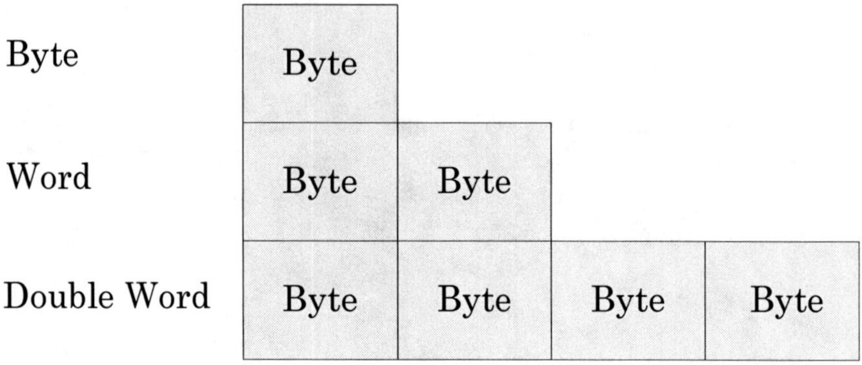

Byte	Byte			
Word	Byte	Byte		
Double Word	Byte	Byte	Byte	Byte

Picture 5.1

Bit Granularity

Every byte consists of 8 bits. Every bit has a value of 0 or 1. Here are some examples of bytes, words and double words shown as bit strings (we can also see clearly the correspondence between 4 bit sequences and hexadecimal numbers, Table 3.1):

- Byte

  C / C++: unsigned char

  Windows definitions: BYTE, UCHAR

  8 bits

  Values 0_{dec} - 255_{dec} or 0_{hex} - FF_{hex}

  Example: 12_{dec} 00001100_{bin} $0C_{hex}$

- Word

  C / C++: unsigned short

  Windows definitions: USHORT, WORD

  16 bits

  Values 0_{dec} - 65535_{dec} or 0_{hex} - $FFFF_{hex}$

  Example: 0000000000001100_{bin} $000C_{hex}$

- Double word

  C / C++: unsigned int, unsigned, unsigned long

  Windows definitions: DWORD, ULONG

  32 bits

  Values 0_{dec} - 4294967295_{dec} or 0_{hex} - $FFFFFFFF_{hex}$

  Example: $00000000000000000000000000001100_{bin}$

  $0000000C_{hex}$

Memory Layout

Minimal addressable element of memory is byte. Maximum address-able element is double word on 32-bit machines and quad word or qword on 64-bit machines. All general registers are 32-bit on 32-bit processors or presented as such when emulating 32-bit mode on 64-bit processors and can contain double word value. Picture 5.2 shows typical memory layout and Picture 5.3 shows byte layout of some general CPU registers.

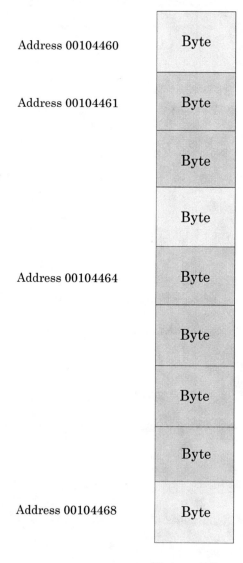

Picture 5.2

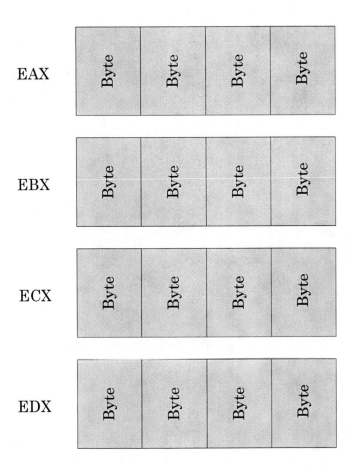

Picture 5.3

Chapter 6: Pointers to Memory

Pointers Revisited

Pointer is a memory cell or a register that contains the address of another memory cell. Memory pointers have their own addresses because they are memory cells too. On 32-bit Windows pointers are always 32-bit. On 64-bit Windows pointers are 64-bit except emulation mode when executing 32-bit applications and services.

Addressing Types

As we have seen in Chapter 5, memory cells can be of one byte, word or double word sizes. Therefore we can have a pointer to a byte (byte ptr), a pointer to a word (word ptr), a pointer to a double word (dword ptr). WinDbg disassembly output in Chapter 4 has byte ptr and dword ptr prefixes in instructions involving pointers to memory.

Here are some illustrated examples:

```
mov byte ptr [eax], 0xFF
```

The layout of memory before instruction execution is shown on Picture 6.1 and the layout of memory after execution is shown on Picture 6.2.

```
mov word ptr [eax], 0xFF

mov dword ptr [eax], 0xFF
```

The layout of memory before instruction execution is shown on Picture 6.3 and the layout of memory after execution is shown on Picture 6.4. We can see that although we specify just one byte 0xFF as a source operand to MOV instruction it replaces all other 3 bytes of a double word in memory because we specify the destination as a pointer to 4 bytes and 0xFF is really 0x000000FF as a double word. So we need to specify dword ptr prefix to disambiguate moving a double word value from moving a byte value. In the following equivalent instruction we don't need to specify dword ptr prefix:

```
mov [eax], 0x000000FF
```

Picture 6.5 shows a summary of various addressing modes.

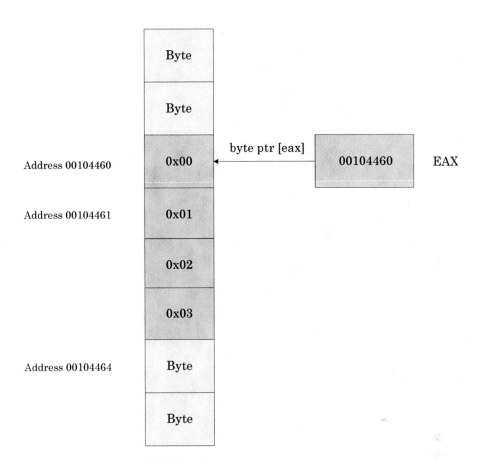

Picture 6.1

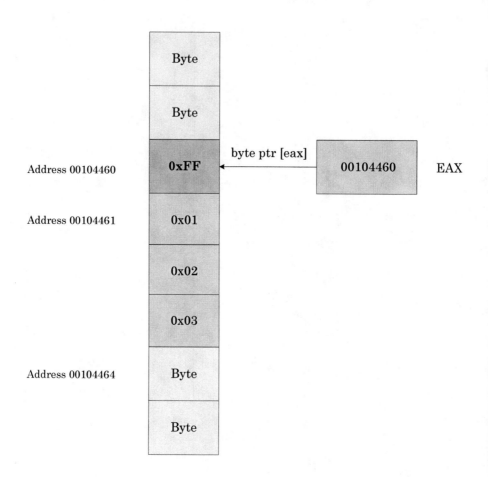

Picture 6.2

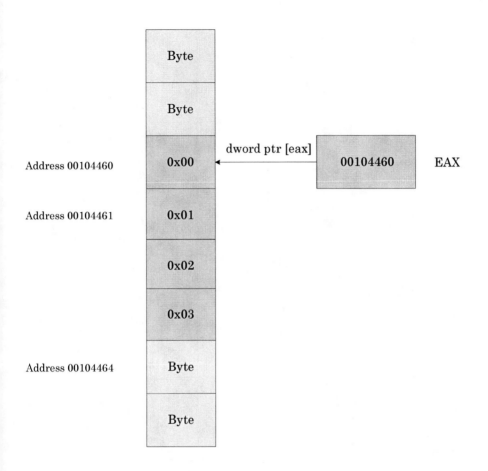

Picture 6.3

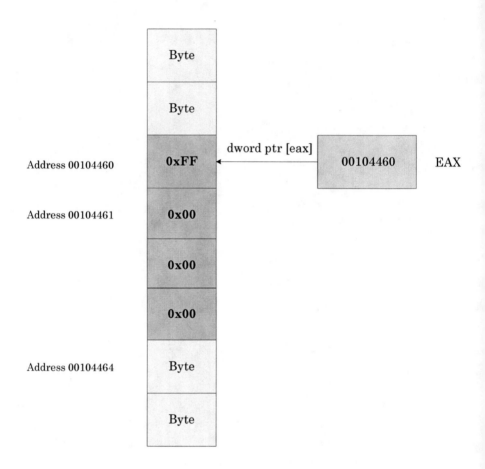

Picture 6.4

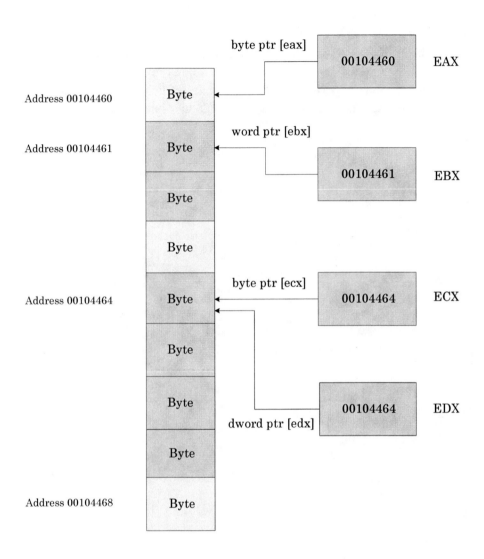

Picture 6.5

Registers Revisited

EAX, EBX, ECX, EDX registers can be used as pointers to memory. EAX and EDX registers contain the multiplication result after executing IMUL instruction. ECX register is often used as a loop counter, E(Counter)X, in assembly language corresponding to simple loops in C and C++ code:

```
for (int i = 0; i < N ; ++i)
```

NULL Pointers

Addresses 0x00000000 – 0x0000FFFF are specifically made inaccessible on Windows. The following code will force an application crash or BSOD if executed inside a driver:

```
mov eax, 0xF

mov [eax], 1  ; Access violation
```

Invalid Pointers

There are different kinds of invalid pointers that cause an access violation when we try to dereference them:

- NULL pointers
- Pointers to inaccessible memory
- Pointers to read-only memory when writing

Other pointers may or may not cause an access violation and some of them will be discussed in subsequent chapters:

- Pointers pointing to "random" memory
- Uninitialized pointers having random value inherited from past code executions
- Dangling pointers

The latter pointers are similar to pointers pointing to "random" memory locations and arise when we forget to set pointer variables to zero (NULL) after disposing of memory they point to. By nullifying pointers we indicate that they no longer point to memory.

Variables as Pointers

Suppose we have the two memory addresses (locations) "a" and "b" declared and defined in C and C++ as:

```
int a, b;
```

These are normal variables "a" and "b". In addition we can have another two memory addresses (locations) "pa" and "pb" declared and defined in C and C++ as:

```
int *pa, *pb;
```

Here pa is a pointer to int or, in another words, the memory cell pa contains the address of another memory cell that contains an integer value.

Pointer Initialization

In order to have pointers to point to memory we need to initialize them with corresponding memory addresses. Here is typical C or C++ code that does this:

```
int a;            // uninitialized variable

int *pa;          // uninitialized pointer

pa = &a;          // [pa] now contains the address a

int b = 12;       // initialized variable

int *pb = &b;     // initialized pointer
```

We can see that pointers are also variables and can change their values effectively pointing to different memory locations during program execution.

Note: Program Sections

A bit of additional information about initialized and uninitialized variables that is useful to know: an executable program on Windows is divided into different sections. Two of them are called .data where all initialized global and static variables (including pointers) are put and .bss (block storage space) where all uninitialized global and static variables (including pointers) are put.

Why do we need different program sections? Consider this C or C++ data definition:

```
int array[1000000]; // size 4,000,000 bytes or 3.815Mb
```

We would expect the size of .EXE file to be about 4Mb. However, the program size on a disk is only 32Kb. This is because the uninitialized array was put into a .bss section that contains only information about its size. When we launch the program this array is recreated from its size information and filled with zeroes. The size of program in memory becomes about 4Mb.

In the case of the initialized array the program size on disk 3.84Mb:

```
int array[1000000] = { 12 };
```

This is because the array was put into a .data section and contains the following sequence of integers { 12, 0, 0, 0, 0 ... }.

More Pseudo Notation

We remind that [a] means contents of memory at the address a, [eax] means contents of memory at the address stored in EAX register (here EAX is a pointer).

We also introduce additional notation we employ in this and subsequent chapters: *[pa] means contents at the address stored at the address pa and is called dereferencing a pointer whose address is pa. The corresponding C code is similar:

```
int *pa = &a;

int b = *pa;
```

"MemoryPointers" Project: Memory Layout

This project is very similar to the "Pointers" project from Chapter 4. We have this data declaration and definition in C or C++ language:

    int a, b;

    int *pa, *pb = &b;

The project code corresponds to the following pseudo-code and assembly language:

[pa] := address a	**lea eax, a**
	mov [pa], eax
*[pa] := 1 ; [a] = 1	mov eax, [pa]
	mov [eax], 1
*[pb] := 1 ; [b] = 1	mov ebx, [pb]
	mov [ebx], 1
*[pb] := *[pb] + *[pa] ; [b] = 2	mov ecx, [eax]
	add ecx, [ebx]
	mov [ebx], ecx

The project for this chapter can be downloaded from:

ftp://dumpanalysis.org/pub/WDPF/Chapter6/

The executable is located under MemoryPointers\Debug subfolder. We can load it into WinDbg and disassemble its main function as described in Chapter 2 or Chapter 4.

First we load MemoryPointers.exe using File\Open Executable... menu option in WinDbg and get the following output:

```
Microsoft (R) Windows Debugger Version 6.9.0003.113 X86
Copyright (c) Microsoft Corporation. All rights reserved.
CommandLine: C:\WDPF\MemoryPointers\Debug\MemoryPointers.exe
```

```
Symbol search path is: *** Invalid ***
**********************************************************************
* Symbol loading may be unreliable without a symbol search path.     *
* Use .symfix to have the debugger choose a symbol path.             *
* After setting your symbol path,                                    *
* use .reload to refresh symbol locations.                           *
**********************************************************************
Executable search path is:
ModLoad: 00400000 00499000    MemoryPointers.exe
ModLoad: 7c900000 7c9b0000    ntdll.dll
ModLoad: 7c800000 7c8f4000    C:\WINDOWS\system32\kernel32.dll
(ea4.ea8): Break instruction exception - code 80000003 (first chance)
eax=00251eb4 ebx=7ffdf000 ecx=00000000 edx=00000001 esi=00251f48
edi=00251eb4
eip=7c901230 esp=0012fb20 ebp=0012fc94 iopl=0         nv up ei pl nz na po nc
cs=001b  ss=0023  ds=0023  es=0023  fs=003b  gs=0000              efl=00000202
*** ERROR: Symbol file could not be found.  Defaulted to export symbols
for ntdll.dll -
ntdll!DbgBreakPoint:
7c901230 cc                  int     3
```

We notice that Symbol search path is invalid and correct this by specifying a location where to put the required symbol files from Microsoft internet symbol server:

```
0:000> .symfix c:\mss
```

Then we put a breakpoint to main function and run the program until WinDbg breaks in:

```
0:000> bp main

0:000> g
Breakpoint 0 hit
eax=00333068 ebx=7ffdf000 ecx=00000001 edx=003330e0 esi=7c9118f1
edi=00011970
eip=0042d620 esp=0012ff70 ebp=0012ffb8 iopl=0         nv up ei pl zr na pe nc
cs=001b  ss=0023  ds=0023  es=0023  fs=003b  gs=0000              efl=00000246
MemoryPointers!main:
0042d620 55                  push    ebp
```

For visual clarity we disable the output of binary codes before disassembling main function:

```
0:000> .asm no_code_bytes
Assembly options: no_code_bytes


0:000> uf main
MemoryPointers!main [c:\wdpf\memorypointers\memorypointers.cpp @ 5]:
    5 0042d620 push    ebp
    5 0042d621 mov     ebp,esp
    5 0042d623 sub     esp,0C0h
    5 0042d629 push    ebx
    5 0042d62a push    esi
    5 0042d62b push    edi
    5 0042d62c lea     edi,[ebp-0C0h]
    5 0042d632 mov     ecx,30h
    5 0042d637 mov     eax,0CCCCCCCCh
    5 0042d63c rep     stos dword ptr es:[edi]
    8 0042d63e lea     eax,[MemoryPointers!a (004944a8)]
    9 0042d644 mov     dword ptr [MemoryPointers!pa (004944a0)],eax
   11 0042d649 mov     eax,dword ptr [MemoryPointers!pa (004944a0)]
   12 0042d64e mov     byte ptr [eax],1
   14 0042d651 mov     ebx,dword ptr [MemoryPointers!pb (00493000)]
   15 0042d657 mov     byte ptr [ebx],1
   17 0042d65a mov     ecx,dword ptr [eax]
   18 0042d65c add     ecx,dword ptr [ebx]
   20 0042d65e mov     dword ptr [ebx],ecx
   23 0042d660 xor     eax,eax
   24 0042d662 pop     edi
   24 0042d663 pop     esi
   24 0042d664 pop     ebx
   24 0042d665 add     esp,0C0h
   24 0042d66b cmp     ebp,esp
   24 0042d66d call    MemoryPointers!ILT+3395(__RTC_CheckEsp) (0042bd48)
   24 0042d672 mov     esp,ebp
   24 0042d674 pop     ebp
   24 0042d675 ret
```

Because our real project code starts with LEA instruction we find its code address in the listing above, set a breakpoint on it and resume our program execution:

```
0:000> bp 0042d63e


0:000> g
Breakpoint 1 hit
eax=cccccccc ebx=7ffdf000 ecx=00000000 edx=003330e0 esi=7c9118f1
edi=0012ff6c
eip=0042d63e esp=0012fea0 ebp=0012ff6c iopl=0         nv up ei pl nz na pe nc
cs=001b  ss=0023  ds=0023  es=0023  fs=003b  gs=0000          efl=00000206
MemoryPointers!main+0x1e:
0042d63e lea       eax,[MemoryPointers!a (004944a8)]
```

Then we clear EAX, EBX and ECX registers to set up memory layout that is easy to follow:

```
0:000> r eax = 0


0:000> r ebx = 0


0:000> r ecx = 0


0:000> r
eax=00000000 ebx=00000000 ecx=00000000 edx=003330e0 esi=7c9118f1
edi=0012ff6c
eip=0042d63e esp=0012fea0 ebp=0012ff6c iopl=0         nv up ei pl nz na pe nc
cs=001b  ss=0023  ds=0023  es=0023  fs=003b  gs=0000          efl=00000206
MemoryPointers!main+0x1e:
0042d63e lea       eax,[MemoryPointers!a (004944a8)]
```

We check the values and addresses of a, b, pa and pb variables:

```
0:000> dc MemoryPointers!a l1
004944a8  00000000                            ....


0:000> dc MemoryPointers!b l1
004944a4  00000000                            ....


0:000> dc MemoryPointers!pa l1
004944a0  00000000                            ....


0:000> dc MemoryPointers!pb l1
00493000  004944a4
```

This corresponds to the memory layout before executing the first LEA instruction and it is shown on Picture 6.6.

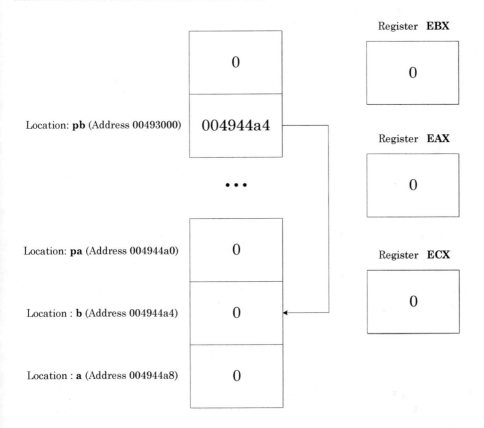

Picture 6.6

We then execute our code step by step. Changes in registers and memory are highlighted in bold.

```
[From previous output]
eax=00000000 ebx=00000000 ecx=00000000 edx=003330e0 esi=7c9118f1
edi=0012ff6c
eip=0042d63e esp=0012fea0 ebp=0012ff6c iopl=0       nv up ei pl nz na pe nc
cs=001b  ss=0023  ds=0023  es=0023  fs=003b  gs=0000           efl=00000206
MemoryPointers!main+0x1e:
0042d63e lea     eax,[MemoryPointers!a (004944a8)]
```

```
0:000> t

eax=004944a8 ebx=00000000 ecx=00000000 edx=003330e0 esi=7c9118f1
edi=0012ff6c
eip=0042d644 esp=0012fea0 ebp=0012ff6c iopl=0         nv up ei pl nz na pe nc
cs=001b  ss=0023  ds=0023  es=0023  fs=003b  gs=0000             efl=00000206
MemoryPointers!main+0x24:
0042d644 mov     dword ptr [MemoryPointers!pa (004944a0)],eax
ds:0023:004944a0=00000000


0:000> dc MemoryPointers!pa l1
004944a0  004944a8                            .DI.


0:000> t

eax=004944a8 ebx=00000000 ecx=00000000 edx=003330e0 esi=7c9118f1
edi=0012ff6c
eip=0042d649 esp=0012fea0 ebp=0012ff6c iopl=0         nv up ei pl nz na pe nc
cs=001b  ss=0023  ds=0023  es=0023  fs=003b  gs=0000             efl=00000206
MemoryPointers!main+0x29:
0042d649 mov     eax,dword ptr [MemoryPointers!pa (004944a0)]
ds:0023:004944a0={MemoryPointers!a (004944a8)}


0:000> t

eax=004944a8 ebx=00000000 ecx=00000000 edx=003330e0 esi=7c9118f1
edi=0012ff6c
eip=0042d64e esp=0012fea0 ebp=0012ff6c iopl=0         nv up ei pl nz na pe nc
cs=001b  ss=0023  ds=0023  es=0023  fs=003b  gs=0000             efl=00000206
MemoryPointers!main+0x2e:
0042d64e mov     byte ptr [eax],1


0:000> t

eax=004944a8 ebx=00000000 ecx=00000000 edx=003330e0 esi=7c9118f1
edi=0012ff6c
eip=0042d651 esp=0012fea0 ebp=0012ff6c iopl=0         nv up ei pl nz na pe nc
cs=001b  ss=0023  ds=0023  es=0023  fs=003b  gs=0000             efl=00000206
MemoryPointers!main+0x31:
0042d651 mov     ebx,dword ptr [MemoryPointers!pb (00493000)]
ds:0023:00493000={MemoryPointers!b (004944a4)}


0:000> dc @eax l1
004944a8  00000001                            ....
```

```
0:000> dc MemoryPointers!a l1
004944a8  00000001                          ....

0:000> t

eax=004944a8 ebx=004944a4 ecx=00000000 edx=003330e0 esi=7c9118f1
edi=0012ff6c
eip=0042d657 esp=0012fea0 ebp=0012ff6c iopl=0         nv up ei pl nz na pe nc
cs=001b  ss=0023  ds=0023  es=0023  fs=003b  gs=0000            efl=00000206
MemoryPointers!main+0x37:
0042d657 mov     byte ptr [ebx],1                ds:0023:004944a4=00


0:000> t
eax=004944a8 ebx=004944a4 ecx=00000000 edx=003330e0 esi=7c9118f1
edi=0012ff6c
eip=0042d65a esp=0012fea0 ebp=0012ff6c iopl=0         nv up ei pl nz na pe nc
cs=001b  ss=0023  ds=0023  es=0023  fs=003b  gs=0000            efl=00000206
MemoryPointers!main+0x3a:
0042d65a mov     ecx,dword ptr [eax]            ds:0023:004944a8=00000001


0:000> dc MemoryPointers!b l1
004944a4  00000001                          ....

0:000> dc @ebx l1
004944a4  00000001                          ....

0:000> t
eax=004944a8 ebx=004944a4 ecx=00000001 edx=003330e0 esi=7c9118f1
edi=0012ff6c
eip=0042d65c esp=0012fea0 ebp=0012ff6c iopl=0         nv up ei pl nz na pe nc
cs=001b  ss=0023  ds=0023  es=0023  fs=003b  gs=0000            efl=00000206
MemoryPointers!main+0x3c:
0042d65c add     ecx,dword ptr [ebx]            ds:0023:004944a4=00000001


0:000> t
eax=004944a8 ebx=004944a4 ecx=00000002 edx=003330e0 esi=7c9118f1
edi=0012ff6c
eip=0042d65e esp=0012fea0 ebp=0012ff6c iopl=0         nv up ei pl nz na po nc
cs=001b  ss=0023  ds=0023  es=0023  fs=003b  gs=0000            efl=00000202
MemoryPointers!main+0x3e:
0042d65e mov     dword ptr [ebx],ecx            ds:0023:004944a4=00000001
```

```
0:000> t
eax=004944a8 ebx=004944a4 ecx=00000002 edx=003330e0 esi=7c9118f1
edi=0012ff6c
eip=0042d660 esp=0012fea0 ebp=0012ff6c iopl=0        nv up ei pl nz na po nc
cs=001b  ss=0023  ds=0023  es=0023  fs=003b  gs=0000            efl=00000202
MemoryPointers!main+0x40:
0042d660 xor      eax,eax


0:000> dc MemoryPointers!b l1
004944a4  00000002                             ....


0:000> dc @ebx l1
004944a4  00000002
```

Final memory layout and registers are shown on Picture 6.7.

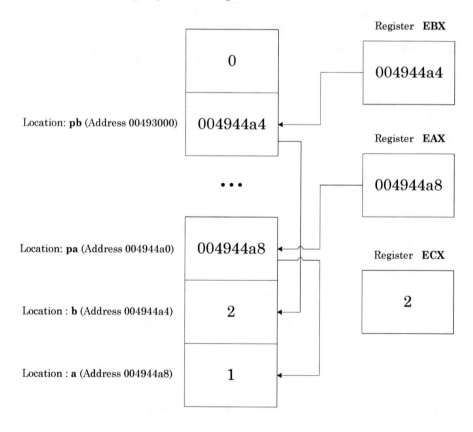

Picture 6.7

Chapter 7: Logical Instructions and EIP

Instruction Format

We have seen that assembly language instructions have uniform format:

Opcode *operand*

Opcode *destination_operand, source_operand*

Operands can be registers (reg), memory reference (mem) or some number, called immediate value (imm). Typical notational examples:

```
inc mem/reg

dec mem/reg

add mem/reg, reg/imm

add reg, mem/imm
```

and some concrete assembly language examples:

```
inc dword ptr [eax]

dec byte ptr [a]

add byte ptr [eax], 10

add eax, dword ptr [a]
```

Logical Shift Instructions

In addition to arithmetic instructions there are so called logical shift instructions that just shift bit string to the left or to the right.

Shift to the left:

```
11111111   ->   11111110   ; shift by 1

11111110   ->   11110000   ; shift by 3

shl   mem/reg, imm/reg

shl eax, 1

shl byte ptr [eax], ecx
```

Shift to the right:

```
11111111   ->   01111111   ; shift by 1

01111111   ->   00001111   ; shift by 3

shr   mem/reg, imm/reg

shr eax, 1

shr byte ptr [eax], ecx
```

Logical Operations

Here we recall logical operations and corresponding truth tables you probably learned earlier. Here we abbreviate True as T and False as F.

AND

```
1 and 1 = 1    T and T = T

1 and 0 = 0    T and F = F

0 and 1 = 0    F and T = F

0 and 0 = 0    F and F = F
```

OR

```
1 or 1 = 1    T or T = T

1 or 0 = 1    T or F = T

0 or 1 = 1    F or T = T

0 or 0 = 0    F or F = F
```

Zeroing Memory or Registers

There are several ways put a zero value into a register or a memory location:

1. Move a value:

    ```
    mov dword ptr [a], 0

    mov eax, 0
    ```

2. Use XOR (Exclusive OR) logical operation:

    ```
    xor eax, eax
    ```

    XOR

    1 xor 1 = 0   T xor T = F

    1 xor 0 = 1   T xor F = T

    0 xor 1 = 1   F xor T = T

    0 xor 0 = 0   F xor F = F

This operation clears its destination operand because the source operand is the same and the same bits are cleared.

Instruction Pointer

Consider these two execution steps from the previous chapter project:

```
0:000> t
eax=004944a8 ebx=004944a4 ecx=00000002 edx=003330e0 esi=7c9118f1
edi=0012ff6c
eip=0042d65e esp=0012fea0 ebp=0012ff6c iopl=0         nv up ei pl nz na po nc
cs=001b  ss=0023  ds=0023  es=0023  fs=003b  gs=0000         efl=00000202
MemoryPointers!main+0x3e:
0042d65e mov     dword ptr [ebx],ecx          ds:0023:004944a4=00000001


0:000> t
eax=004944a8 ebx=004944a4 ecx=00000002 edx=003330e0 esi=7c9118f1
edi=0012ff6c
eip=0042d660 esp=0012fea0 ebp=0012ff6c iopl=0         nv up ei pl nz na po nc
cs=001b  ss=0023  ds=0023  es=0023  fs=003b  gs=0000         efl=00000202
MemoryPointers!main+0x40:
0042d660 xor     eax,eax
```

When MOV instruction at 0042d65e address is being executed another CPU register EIP points to the next instruction at 0042d660 address to be executed. This is shown on Picture 7.1.

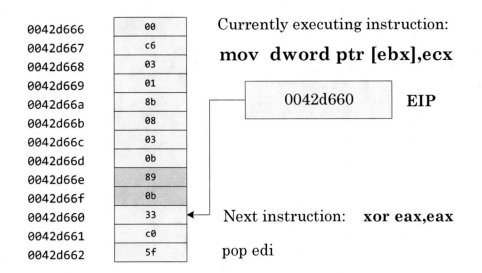

Picture 7.1

Note: Code Section

Recall that in Chapter 6 we discussed .data and .bss sections where program data is put. The program code is put into .text section.

!dh WinDbg command lists various program sections and their information:

```
0:000> !dh MemoryPointers


File Type: EXECUTABLE IMAGE
FILE HEADER VALUES
     14C machine (i386)
       6 number of sections
496F2C7D time date stamp Thu Jan 15 12:30:53 2009

       0 file pointer to symbol table
       0 number of symbols
      E0 size of optional header
     103 characteristics
            Relocations stripped
            Executable
            32 bit word machine


OPTIONAL HEADER VALUES
     10B magic #
    9.00 linker version
   56400 size of code
   16200 size of initialized data
       0 size of uninitialized data
   2BB72 address of entry point
    1000 base of code
         ----- new -----
00400000 image base
    1000 section alignment
     200 file alignment
       3 subsystem (Windows CUI)
    5.00 operating system version
    0.00 image version
    5.00 subsystem version
```

```
   99000 size of image
     400 size of headers
       0 checksum
00100000 size of stack reserve
00001000 size of stack commit
00100000 size of heap reserve
00001000 size of heap commit
       0 [        0] address [size] of Export Directory
   97000 [       28] address [size] of Import Directory
   98000 [      C09] address [size] of Resource Directory
       0 [        0] address [size] of Exception Directory
       0 [        0] address [size] of Security Directory
       0 [        0] address [size] of Base Relocation Directory
   82C50 [       1C] address [size] of Debug Directory
       0 [        0] address [size] of Description Directory
       0 [        0] address [size] of Special Directory
       0 [        0] address [size] of Thread Storage Directory
       0 [        0] address [size] of Load Configuration Directory
       0 [        0] address [size] of Bound Import Directory
   97214 [      1EC] address [size] of Import Address Table Directory
       0 [        0] address [size] of Delay Import Directory
       0 [        0] address [size] of COR20 Header Directory
       0 [        0] address [size] of Reserved Directory


[Skipped]


SECTION HEADER #2
   .text name
   56391 virtual size
   2B000 virtual address
   56400 size of raw data
     400 file pointer to raw data
       0 file pointer to relocation table
       0 file pointer to line numbers
       0 number of relocations
       0 number of line numbers
60000020 flags
         Code
         (no align specified)
         Execute Read
```

[Skipped]

Debug Directories(1)

         Type   Size   Address   Pointer
         cv   48   912d4   65ad4 Format: RSDS, guid, 2,
c:\WDPF\MemoryPointers\Debug\MemoryPointers.pdb

SECTION HEADER #4
    .data name
     37F0 virtual size
    93000 virtual address
     1600 size of raw data
    67600 file pointer to raw data
        0 file pointer to relocation table
        0 file pointer to line numbers
        0 number of relocations
        0 number of line numbers
C0000040 flags
         Initialized Data
         (no align specified)
         Read Write

[Skipped]

Chapter 8: Reconstructing a Program with Pointers

Example of Disassembly Output: No Optimization

The ability to reconstruct approximate C or C++ code from code disassembly is very important in memory dump analysis and debugging.

The project for this chapter can be downloaded from:

ftp://dumpanalysis.org/pub/WDPF/Chapter8/

The executable is located under PointersAsVariables\Debug subfolder. We load it into WinDbg and disassemble its main function.

First we load PointersAsVariables.exe using File\Open Executable... menu option in WinDbg and get the following output:

```
Microsoft (R) Windows Debugger Version 6.9.0003.113 X86
Copyright (c) Microsoft Corporation. All rights reserved.
CommandLine: C:\WDPF\PointersAsVariables\Debug\PointersAsVariables.exe
Symbol search path is: *** Invalid ***
************************************************************************
* Symbol loading may be unreliable without a symbol search path.       *
* Use .symfix to have the debugger choose a symbol path.               *
* After setting your symbol path,                                      *
* use .reload to refresh symbol locations.                            *
************************************************************************
Executable search path is:
ModLoad: 00400000 00499000   PointersAsVariables.exe
ModLoad: 7c900000 7c9b0000   ntdll.dll
ModLoad: 7c800000 7c8f4000   C:\WINDOWS\system32\kernel32.dll
(514.148): Break instruction exception - code 80000003 (first chance)
eax=00251eb4 ebx=7ffdd000 ecx=00000000 edx=00000001 esi=00251f48
edi=00251eb4
eip=7c901230 esp=0012fb20 ebp=0012fc94 iopl=0         nv up ei pl nz na po nc
cs=001b  ss=0023  ds=0023  es=0023  fs=003b  gs=0000              efl=00000202
*** ERROR: Symbol file could not be found.  Defaulted to export symbols
for ntdll.dll -
ntdll!DbgBreakPoint:
7c901230 cc                  int     3
```

We notice that Symbol search path is invalid and correct this by specifying a location where to put the required symbol files from Microsoft internet symbol server:

```
0:000> .symfix c:\mss
```

Then we put a breakpoint to main function and run the program until WinDbg breaks in:

```
0:000> bp main


0:000> g
Breakpoint 0 hit
eax=00333078 ebx=7ffdd000 ecx=00000001 edx=003330f8 esi=7c9118f1
edi=00011970
eip=0042d600 esp=0012ff70 ebp=0012ffb8 iopl=0         nv up ei pl zr na pe nc
cs=001b  ss=0023  ds=0023  es=0023  fs=003b  gs=0000          efl=00000246
PointersAsVariables!main:
0042d600 55              push    ebp
```

Next we disassemble our main function:

```
0:000> .asm no_code_bytes
Assembly options: no_code_bytes


0:000> uf main
PointersAsVariables!main
[c:\wdpf\pointersasvariables\pointersasvariables.cpp @ 5]:
    5 0042d600 push    ebp
    5 0042d601 mov     ebp,esp
    5 0042d603 sub     esp,0C0h
    5 0042d609 push    ebx
    5 0042d60a push    esi
    5 0042d60b push    edi
    5 0042d60c lea     edi,[ebp-0C0h]
    5 0042d612 mov     ecx,30h
    5 0042d617 mov     eax,0CCCCCCCCh
    5 0042d61c rep stos dword ptr es:[edi]
    6 0042d61e mov     dword ptr [PointersAsVariables!pa (004944a0)],
offset PointersAsVariables!a (004944a8)
    7 0042d628 mov     dword ptr [PointersAsVariables!pb (004944ac)],
offset PointersAsVariables!b (004944a4)
    9 0042d632 mov     eax,dword ptr [PointersAsVariables!pa (004944a0)]
    9 0042d637 mov     dword ptr [eax],1
```

```
10 0042d63d mov     eax,dword ptr [PointersAsVariables!pb (004944ac)]
10 0042d642 mov     dword ptr [eax],1
12 0042d648 mov     eax,dword ptr [PointersAsVariables!pb (004944ac)]
12 0042d64d mov     ecx,dword ptr [eax]
12 0042d64f mov     edx,dword ptr [PointersAsVariables!pa (004944a0)]
12 0042d655 add     ecx,dword ptr [edx]
12 0042d657 mov     eax,dword ptr [PointersAsVariables!pb (004944ac)]
12 0042d65c mov     dword ptr [eax],ecx
14 0042d65e mov     eax,dword ptr [PointersAsVariables!pb (004944ac)]
14 0042d663 mov     ecx,dword ptr [eax]
14 0042d665 shl     ecx,1
14 0042d667 mov     edx,dword ptr [PointersAsVariables!pb (004944ac)]
14 0042d66d mov     dword ptr [edx],ecx
16 0042d66f xor     eax,eax
17 0042d671 pop     edi
17 0042d672 pop     esi
17 0042d673 pop     ebx
17 0042d674 mov     esp,ebp
17 0042d676 pop     ebp
17 0042d677 ret
```

Reconstructing C/C++ Code: Part 1

Now we go from instruction to instruction and try to reconstruct pseudo-code which is shown as comments to assembly language code.

```
mov     dword ptr [PointersAsVariables!pa (004944a0)],offset
PointersAsVariables!a (004944a8)
; [pa]   := address of a
mov     dword ptr [PointersAsVariables!pb (004944ac)],offset
PointersAsVariables!b (004944a4)
; [pb]   := address of b
mov     eax,dword ptr [PointersAsVariables!pa (004944a0)]
; eax    := [pa]
mov     dword ptr [eax],1
; [eax]  := 1
mov     eax,dword ptr [PointersAsVariables!pb (004944ac)]
; eax    := [pb]
mov     dword ptr [eax],1
; [eax]  := 1
mov     eax,dword ptr [PointersAsVariables!pb (004944ac)]
; eax    := [pb]
mov     ecx,dword ptr [eax]
; ecx    := [eax]
mov     edx,dword ptr [PointersAsVariables!pa (004944a0)]
; edx    := [pa]
add     ecx,dword ptr [edx]
; ecx    := ecx + [edx]
mov     eax,dword ptr [PointersAsVariables!pb (004944ac)]
; eax    := [pb]
```

```
mov      dword ptr [eax],ecx
; [eax] := ecx
mov      eax,dword ptr [PointersAsVariables!pb (004944ac)]
; eax    := [pb]
mov      ecx,dword ptr [eax]
; ecx    := [eax]
shl      ecx,1
; ecx    := ecx * 2
mov      edx,dword ptr [PointersAsVariables!pb (004944ac)]
; edx    := [pb]
mov      dword ptr [edx],ecx
; [edx]  := ecx
```

Reconstructing C/C++ Code: Part 2

Now we group pseudo-code together with possible mixed C/C++ and assembly language equivalents:

```
[pa]   := address of a          ;   int a, b; int *pa, *pb;

[pb]   := address of b          ;   pa = &a; pb = &b;

eax    := [pa]                  ;   *pa = 1;
[eax]  := 1

eax    := [pb]                  ;   *pb = 1;
[eax]  := 1

eax    := [pb]                  ;   ecx = *pb;
ecx    := [eax]

edx    := [pa]                  ;   ecx = ecx + *pa;
ecx    := ecx + [edx]

eax    := [pb]                  ;   *pb = ecx;
[eax]  := ecx

eax    := [pb]                  ;   ecx = *pb;
ecx    := [eax]

ecx    := ecx * 2               ;   ecx = ecx * 2;

edx    := [pb]                  ;   *pb = ecx;
[edx]  := ecx
```

Reconstructing C/C++ Code: Part 3

Next we combine more mixed statements into C/C++ language code:

```
int a, b;
int *pa, *pb;

pa = &a;
pb = &b;

*pa = 1;
*pb = 1;

ecx = *pb;
ecx = ecx + *pa;
*pb = ecx;                  ; *pb = *pb + *pa;

ecx = *pb;
ecx = ecx * 2;             ; *pb = *pb * 2;
*pb = ecx;
```

Reconstructing C/C++ Code: C/C++ program

Finally we have something that looks like complete C/C++ code:

```
int a, b;
int *pa, *pb;

pa = &a;
pb = &b;

*pa = 1;
*pb = 1;

*pb = *pb + *pa;
*pb = *pb * 2;
```

If we look at the project source code PointersAsVariables.cpp we would see exactly the same code that was compiled into our executable file that we were disassembling.

Example of Disassembly Output: Optimized Program

Fully optimized program from Release project folder contains less CPU instructions as can be seen from the disassembly:

```
0:000> uf main
PointersAsVariables!main
[c:\wdpf\pointersasvariables\pointersasvariables.cpp @ 5]:
    5 00401000 mov     dword ptr [PointersAsVariables!pa (0040ac60)],
offset PointersAsVariables!a (0040ac68)
    7 0040100a mov     dword ptr [PointersAsVariables!pb (0040ac6c)],
offset PointersAsVariables!b (0040ac64)
    9 00401014 mov     dword ptr [PointersAsVariables!a (0040ac68)],1
   14 0040101e mov     dword ptr [PointersAsVariables!b (0040ac64)],4
   16 00401028 xor     eax,eax
   17 0040102a ret
```

We see that Visual C++ compiler was able to figure out the result of computation: a = 1; b = 4; However one question remains why the compiler did not optimize away the first two instructions initializing pa and pb variables? The answer lies in the nature of separate compilation model in C and C++. We can compile several compilation units (.c or .cpp) files separately and independently. Therefore there is no guarantee that another compilation unit would not reference our statically declared and defined pa and pb variables.

Chapter 9: Memory and Stacks

Stack: A Definition

A stack is a simple computational device with two operations, push and pop, that allows us to pile up data to remember it in LIFO (Last In First Out) manner and help in easy retrieval of the last piled data item as shown on Picture 9.1.

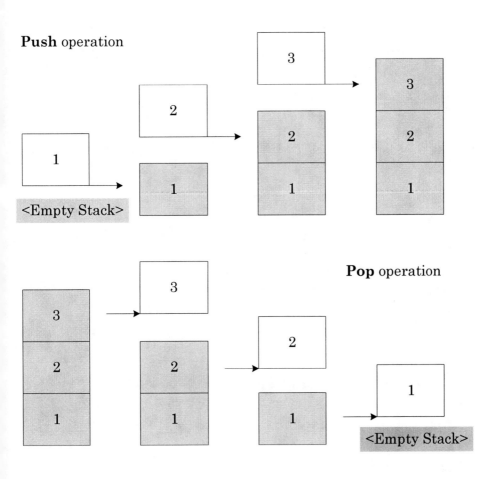

Picture 9.1

Stack Implementation in Memory

CPU ESP register (Stack Pointer) points to the top of stack. As shown on Picture 9.2 the stack grows towards lower memory addresses with every push instruction and this is implemented as ESP register decrement by 4. We can read the top stack value using the following instruction: mov eax, [esp].

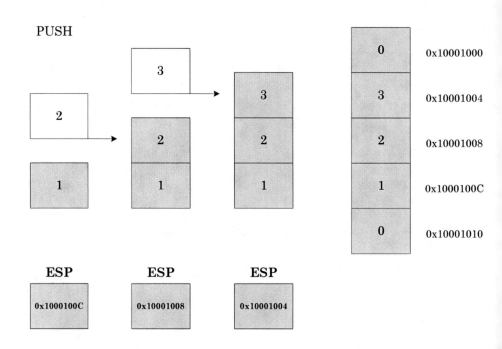

Picture 9.2

The opposite POP instruction increments the value of ESP register as shown on Picture 9.3.

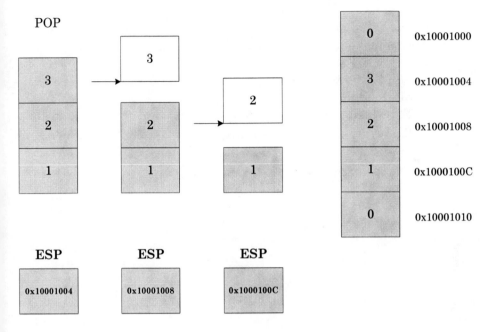

Picture 9.3

Things to Remember

Here is the summary of what we have learnt about stacks with the last 3 points covered in the subsequent chapters of this book:

- Stack operations are LIFO – Last In First Out
- Stack grows down in memory
- ESP register points to the top of a stack
- Stacks are used to store return address for CALL instructions
- Stacks are used to pass parameters to functions
- Stacks are used to store local and temporary variables

PUSH Instruction

We can push a value stored in a register, a value stored at a memory address or a constant (immediate operand):

PUSH r/mem/imm

Here is PUSH simplified pseudo-code adopted from Intel manual:

```
IF OperandSize = 32
      THEN
              ESP := ESP - 4
              [ESP] := OperandValue   ; double word
      ELSE
              ESP := ESP - 2
              [ESP] := OperandValue   ; word
FI
```

Examples:

```
push    eax

push    dword ptr [ebx]

push    byte ptr [ecx]

push    0
```

POP instruction

We can pop a value stored on the top of a stack to a register or to a memory address:

POP r/mem

Here is POP simplified pseudo-code adopted from Intel manual:

```
IF OperandSize = 32
      THEN
              OperandValue := [ESP] ; double word
              ESP := ESP + 4
      ELSE
              OperandValue := [ESP] ; word
              ESP := ESP + 2
FI
```

Examples:

```
pop    eax

pop    dword ptr [ebx]

pop    byte ptr [ecx]
```

Register Review

So far we have seen and used general purpose CPU registers:

- EAX (among its specific uses are to contain function return values and the lower part of a multiplication result)
- EBX
- ECX (among its specific uses is a loop counter)
- EDX (among its specific uses is to contain the higher part of a multiplication result if it exceed maximum 32-bit value)
- EIP (Instruction Pointer)
- ESP (Stack Pointer)

Application Memory Simplified

When an executable file is loaded into memory its header and sections are mapped to memory pages. Some data and code are copied unmodified but some data is initialized and expanded from uninitialized data section. The first stack is also created at this stage. EIP register is set to point to the first program instruction and ESP points to the top of the stack. This simplified process is shown on Picture 9.4

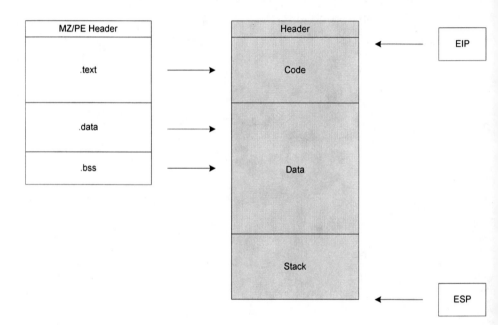

Picture 9.4

Stack Overflow

By default stack size is 1Mb (compiler dependent). This limit can be changed by linker /STACK option or done via Visual C++ project Linker \ System options as show on Picture 9.5.

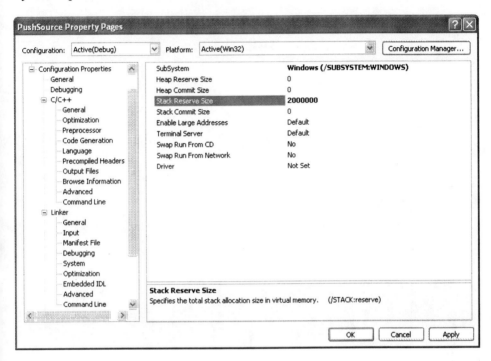

Picture 9.5

If stack grows beyond the reserve limit then stack overflow exception occurs (exception code C00000FD). This might be caused by an unlimited recursion or very deep recursion:

```
int func()
{
        func();
        return 0;
}
```

or very large local variables:

```
int func()
{
        int array[1000000] = { 1  };
        printf("%d", array[1000000-1]);
        // use array to prevent the compiler to optimize it away
}
```

Jumps

Another instruction we need to know and understand before we look deeper into C and C++ functions is called is JMP (Jump). Picture 9.6 shows instructions in memory and corresponding values of EIP register.

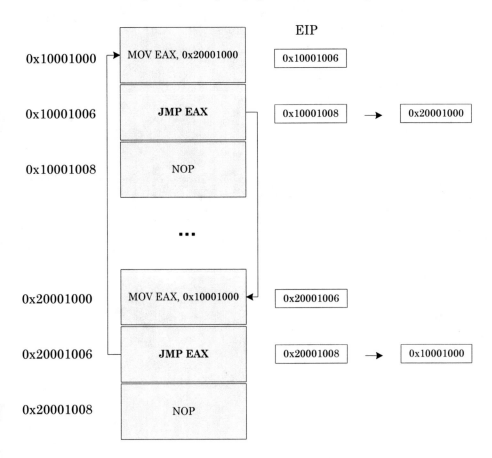

Picture 9.6

We see that JMP instruction changes EIP to point to another memory address and the program execution continues from this location. The code shown on Picture 9.6 loops indefinitely: this can be considered as a hang.

Here is a pseudo-code for absolute JMP instructions adopted from Intel manuals and some examples:

```
Format and arguments:

  JMP  r/mem32

Pseudo-code:

  EIP := DEST ; new destination address for execution

Examples:

  JMP  EAX

  JMP  [EAX]
```

The jump is called absolute because we specify full memory addresses and not a relative +/- number to the current EIP value. The latter jump is called relative.

Calls

Now we discuss two very important instructions that make the implementation of C and C++ function calls much easier. They are called CALL and RET. Picture 9.7 shows instructions in memory and corresponding values of EIP and ESP registers.

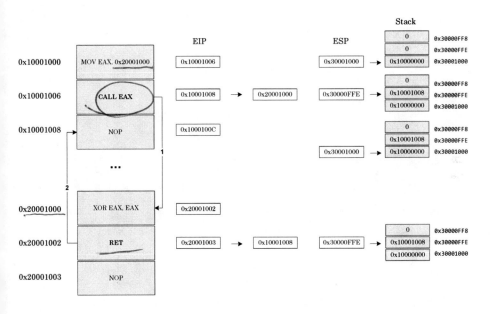

Picture 9.7

We see that CALL instruction pushes the current value of EIP to the stack and changes EIP to point to another memory address. Then the program execution continues from the new location. RET instruction pops the saved EIP value from the stack to EIP register. Then the program execution resumes from the memory location after CALL instruction.

Here is a pseudo-code for absolute CALL instructions and some examples adopted from Intel manuals and some examples:

```
Format and arguments:

    CALL r/mem32

Pseudo-code:

    PUSH (EIP)

    EIP := DEST

Examples:

    CALL EAX

    CALL [EAX]
```

Here is a pseudo-code for RET instruction adopted from Intel manuals:

```
Format:

    RET

Pseudo-code:

    EIP := POP()
```

Call Stack

If one function (the caller) calls another function (the callee) in C and C++ the resulting code is implemented using CALL instruction and during its execution the return address is saved on the stack. If the callee calls another function the return address is also saved on the stack, and so on. Therefore we have the so called call stack of return addresses. Let's see this with a simple but a trimmed down example.

Suppose we have 3 functions with their code occupying the following addresses:

```
func  0x10001000 - 0x10001100
func2 0x10001101 - 0x10001200
func3 0x10001201 - 0x10001300
```

We also have the following code where func calls func2 and func2 calls func3:

```
void func()
{
    func2();
}
void func2()
{
    func3();
}
```

When func calls func2, the caller return address is pushed to the stack and ESP points to some value in 0x10001000 – 0x10001100 range, say 0x10001000. When func2 calls func3, the caller return address is also pushed to the stack and ESP points to some value in 0x10001101 – 0x10001200 range, say 0x10001180. If we interrupt func3 with a debugger and inspect EIP we would find its value in the range of 0x10001201 – 0x10001300, say 0x10001250. Therefore we have the following memory and register layout shown on Picture 9.8 (usual function prolog is not shown: we will learn about it in the next chapter).

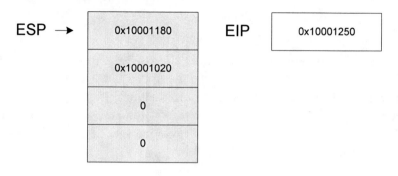

Picture 9.8

The debugger examines the value of EIP and the values on top of the stack and reconstructs this call stack:

```
func3
func2
func
```

The debugger gets address ranges corresponding to func, func2 and func3 from the so called symbol files, which have .PDB extension. This is why we previously used **.symfix** command to download necessary symbol files for our test programs. Projects from ftp also contain .PDB files corresponding to .EXE file to allow WinDbg debugger to understand the memory location of main function, for example.

Exploring Stack in WinDbg

To see call stack in real action we have a project called "SimpleStack" and it can be downloaded from:

ftp://dumpanalysis.org/pub/WDPF/Chapter9/

The executable is located under SimpleStack\Release subfolder. We load SimpleStack.exe using File\Open Executable... menu option in WinDbg and get the following output:

```
Microsoft (R) Windows Debugger Version 6.9.0003.113 X86
Copyright (c) Microsoft Corporation. All rights reserved.


CommandLine: C:\WDPF\SimpleStack\Release\SimpleStack.exe
Symbol search path is: *** Invalid ***
************************************************************************
* Symbol loading may be unreliable without a symbol search path.       *
* Use .symfix to have the debugger choose a symbol path.               *
* After setting your symbol path,                                      *
* use .reload to refresh symbol locations.                            *
************************************************************************
Executable search path is:
ModLoad: 00400000 0040d000   SimpleStack.exe
ModLoad: 7c900000 7c9b0000   ntdll.dll
ModLoad: 7c800000 7c8f4000   C:\WINDOWS\system32\kernel32.dll
(2e0.430): Break instruction exception - code 80000003 (first chance)
eax=00251eb4 ebx=7ffde000 ecx=00000000 edx=00000001 esi=00251f48
edi=00251eb4
eip=7c901230 esp=0012fb20 ebp=0012fc94 iopl=0         nv up ei pl nz na po nc
cs=001b  ss=0023  ds=0023  es=0023  fs=003b  gs=0000             efl=00000202
*** ERROR: Symbol file could not be found.  Defaulted to export symbols
for ntdll.dll -
ntdll!DbgBreakPoint:
7c901230 cc              int     3
```

We notice that Symbol search path is invalid and correct this by specifying a location where to put the required symbol files from Microsoft internet symbol server:

```
0:000> .symfix c:\mss
```

Then we put a breakpoint to main function and run the program until WinDbg breaks in:

```
0:000> bp main

0:000> g
Breakpoint 0 hit
eax=00333058 ebx=7ffde000 ecx=00000001 edx=0040b170 esi=7c9118f1
edi=00011970
eip=00401030 esp=0012ff7c ebp=0012ffc0 iopl=0        nv up ei pl zr na pe nc
cs=001b  ss=0023  ds=0023  es=0023  fs=003b  gs=0000        efl=00000246
SimpleStack!main:
00401030 55                push    ebp
```

The function func3 has a breakpoint instruction inside that allows a debugger to break in and stop the program execution to inspect its state. We resume our program execution from our breakpoint in main function to allow main function to call func, func to call func2, func2 to call func3 and inside func3 to executing the explicit breakpoint:

```
0:000> g
(2e0.430): Break instruction exception - code 80000003 (first chance)
eax=00333058 ebx=7ffde000 ecx=00000001 edx=0040b170 esi=7c9118f1
edi=00011970
eip=00401023 esp=0012ff60 ebp=0012ff60 iopl=0        nv up ei pl zr na pe nc
cs=001b  ss=0023  ds=0023  es=0023  fs=003b  gs=000        efl=00000246
SimpleStack!func3+0x3:
00401023 cc                int     3
```

Now we can inspect the top of the stack:

```
0:000> dd esp
0012ff60   0012ff68 00401018 0012ff70 00401008
0012ff70   0012ff78 00401038 0012ffc0 00401160
0012ff80   00000001 00333008 00333058 3146d38a
0012ff90   00011970 7c9118f1 7ffde000 0012ffac
0012ffa0   7c9118f1 00000000 0012ff8c 4b111360
0012ffb0   0012ffe0 004025d0 3114bf7a 00000000
0012ffc0   0012fff0 7c816d4f 00011970 7c9118f1
0012ffd0   7ffde000 80543dfd 0012ffc8 82249c38
```

The data is meaningless for us so we use another command called **dds** to dump memory with corresponding symbols from PDB files:

```
0:000> dds esp
0012ff60  0012ff68
0012ff64  00401018 SimpleStack!func2+0x8 [c:\wdpf\simplestack\func2.c @ 6]
0012ff68  0012ff70
0012ff6c  00401008 SimpleStack!func+0x8 [c:\wdpf\simplestack\func.c @ 6]
0012ff70  0012ff78
0012ff74  00401038 SimpleStack!main+0x8 [c:\wdpf\simplestack\simplestack.c
@ 6]
0012ff78  0012ffc0
0012ff7c  00401160 SimpleStack!__tmainCRTStartup+0xfb
[f:\dd\vctools\crt_bld\self_x86\crt\src\crt0.c @ 266]
0012ff80  00000001
0012ff84  00333008
0012ff88  00333058
0012ff8c  3146d38a
0012ff90  00011970
0012ff94  7c9118f1 ntdll!RtlDeleteCriticalSection+0x67
0012ff98  7ffde000
0012ff9c  0012ffac
0012ffa0  7c9118f1 ntdll!RtlDeleteCriticalSection+0x67
0012ffa4  00000000
0012ffa8  0012ff8c
0012ffac  4b111360
0012ffb0  0012ffe0
0012ffb4  004025d0 SimpleStack!_except_handler4
0012ffb8  3114bf7a
0012ffbc  00000000
0012ffc0  0012fff0
0012ffc4  7c816d4f kernel32!BaseProcessStart+0x23
0012ffc8  00011970
0012ffcc  7c9118f1 ntdll!RtlDeleteCriticalSection+0x67
0012ffd0  7ffde000
0012ffd4  80543dfd
0012ffd8  0012ffc8
0012ffdc  82249c38
```

The current value of EIP points to func3 and return addresses on the stack are shown in bold. WinDbg is able to reconstruct the following call stack or stack trace:

```
0:000> k

ChildEBP RetAddr
0012ff60 00401018 SimpleStack!func3+0x3 [c:\wdpf\simplestack\func3.c @ 3]
0012ff68 00401008 SimpleStack!func2+0x8 [c:\wdpf\simplestack\func2.c @ 6]
0012ff70 00401038 SimpleStack!func+0x8 [c:\wdpf\simplestack\func.c @ 6]
0012ff78 00401160 SimpleStack!main+0x8 [c:\wdpf\simplestack\simplestack.c
@ 6]
0012ffc0 7c816d4f SimpleStack!__tmainCRTStartup+0xfb
[f:\dd\vctools\crt_bld\self_x86\crt\src\crt0.c @ 266]
0012fff0 00000000 kernel32!BaseProcessStart+0x23
```

Chapter 10: Frame Pointer and Local Variables

Stack Usage

In addition to storage for return address of CALL instructions stack is used to pass parameters to functions and store local variables. Stack is also used to save and restore values held in registers when we want to preserve them during some computation or across function calls. For example, suppose we want to do a multiplication but at the same time we have another valuable data in register EAX and EDX. The multiplication result will overwrite EAX and EDX values and we temporarily put their values on stack:

```
mov     eax, 10
mov     edx, 20
...

...

...                 ; now we want to preserve EAX and EDX
push    eax
push    edx
imul    eax, edx
mov     dword ptr [result], eax
pop     edx     ; pop in reverse order
pop     eax     ; stack is LIFO
```

Register Review

So far we have encountered these general purpose registers:

- EAX (among its specific uses are to contain function return values and the lower part of a multiplication result)
- EBX
- ECX (among its specific uses is a loop counter)
- EDX (among its specific uses is to contain the higher part of a multiplication result if it exceed maximum 32-bit value)
- EIP (Instruction Pointer, points to the next instruction to be executed)
- ESP (Stack Pointer, points to the top of the stack)

Now we come to the next important register on 32-bit platforms called Base Pointer register or sometimes as Stack Frame Pointer register:

EBP

Addressing Array Elements

We can also consider stack memory as an array of memory cells and often EBP register is used to address stack memory elements in the way shown on Picture 10.1 where it slides through the frame of stack memory called stack frame.

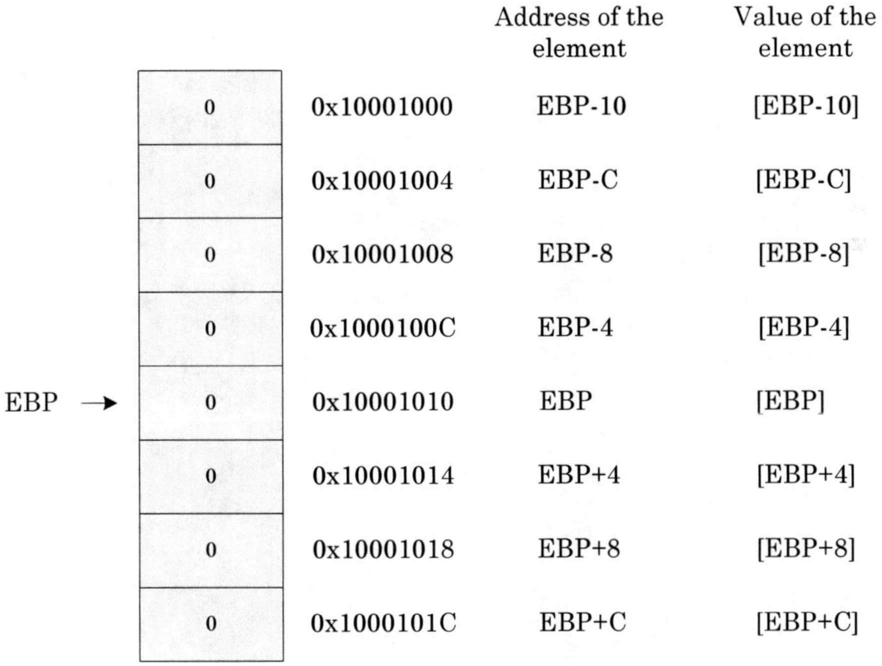

		Address of the element	Value of the element
	0	0x10001000	EBP-10	[EBP-10]
	0	0x10001004	EBP-C	[EBP-C]
	0	0x10001008	EBP-8	[EBP-8]
	0	0x1000100C	EBP-4	[EBP-4]
EBP →	0	0x10001010	EBP	[EBP]
	0	0x10001014	EBP+4	[EBP+4]
	0	0x10001018	EBP+8	[EBP+8]
	0	0x1000101C	EBP+C	[EBP+C]

Picture 10.1

Stack Structure (No Function Parameters)

Suppose the following function is called:

```
void func()
{
        int var1, var2;
        // Body Code
        // ...
}
```

Before the function body code is executed the following pointers are set up:

- [EBP] contains previous EBP
- [EBP-4] contains Local Var 1 (DWORD)
- [EBP-8] contains Local Var 2 (DWORD)

This is illustrated on Picture 10.2.

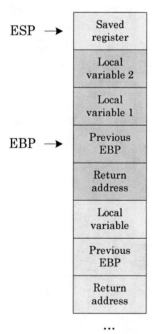

Picture 10.2

Raw Stack (No Local Variables and Function Parameters)

Now we can understand additional data that appear on the raw stack together with function return addresses that we saw in Chapter 9 project "SimpleStack":

```
0:000> r
eax=00333058 ebx=7ffde000 ecx=00000001 edx=0040b170 esi=7c9118f1
edi=00011970
eip=00401023 esp=0012ff60 ebp=0012ff60 iopl=0         nv up ei pl zr na pe nc
cs=001b  ss=0023  ds=0023  es=0023  fs=003b  gs=0000          efl=00000246
SimpleStack!func3+0x3:
00401023 cc              int     3


0:000> dds esp
0012ff60  0012ff68
0012ff64  00401018 SimpleStack!func2+0x8 [c:\wdpf\simplestack\func2.c @ 6]
0012ff68  0012ff70
0012ff6c  00401008 SimpleStack!func+0x8 [c:\wdpf\simplestack\func.c @ 6]
0012ff70  0012ff78
0012ff74  00401038 SimpleStack!main+0x8 [c:\wdpf\simplestack\simplestack.c
@ 6]
0012ff78  0012ffc0
0012ff7c  00401160 SimpleStack!__tmainCRTStartup+0xfb
[f:\dd\vctools\crt_bld\self_x86\crt\src\crt0.c @ 266]
0012ff80  00000001
0012ff84  00333008
0012ff88  00333058
```

Function Prolog

The sequence of instructions resulting in the initialization of EBP register and making the room for local variables is called function prolog. One example of it is shown on Picture 10.3 where func calls func2 which has one local variable var. Sometimes saving necessary registers is also considered as the part of the function prolog.

func() { func2(); }   func2() { int var; }

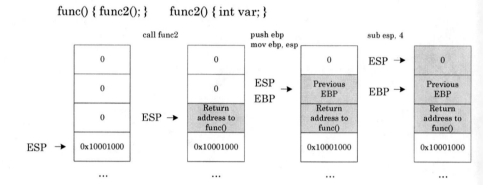

Picture 10.3

Function Epilog

Before the function code makes a return to the caller it must restore the previous value of EBP register to allow the caller to continue addressing its own stack frame properly. This sequence of instructions is called function epilog and it is shown on Picture 10.4.

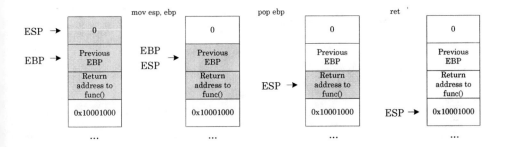

Picture 10.4

"Local Variables" Project

The project for this chapter can be downloaded from:

ftp://dumpanalysis.org/pub/WDPF/Chapter10/

The executable is located under LocalVariables\Debug subfolder. We load it into WinDbg and disassemble its main function.

First we load LocalVariables.exe using File\Open Executable... menu option in WinDbg and get the following output:

```
Microsoft (R) Windows Debugger Version 6.9.0003.113 X86
Copyright (c) Microsoft Corporation. All rights reserved.


CommandLine: C:\WDPF\LocalVariables\Debug\LocalVariables.exe
Symbol search path is: *** Invalid
***************************************************************************
* Symbol loading may be unreliable without a symbol search path.          *
* Use .symfix to have the debugger choose a symbol path.                   *
* After setting your symbol path,                                          *
* use .reload to refresh symbol locations.                                 *
***************************************************************************
Executable search path is:
ModLoad: 00400000 00499000   LocalVariables.exe
ModLoad: 7c900000 7c9b0000   ntdll.dll
ModLoad: 7c800000 7c8f4000   C:\WINDOWS\system32\kernel32.dll
(194.d64): Break instruction exception - code 80000003 (first chance)
eax=00251eb4 ebx=7ffd7000 ecx=00000000 edx=00000001 esi=00251f48
edi=00251eb4
eip=7c901230 esp=0012fb20 ebp=0012fc94 iopl=0         nv up ei pl nz na po nc
cs=001b  ss=0023  ds=0023  es=0023  fs=003b  gs=0000              efl=00000202
*** ERROR: Symbol file could not be found.  Defaulted to export symbols
for ntdll.dll -
ntdll!DbgBreakPoint:
7c901230 cc                 int     3
```

We notice that Symbol search path is invalid and correct this by specifying a location where to put the required symbol files from Microsoft internet symbol server:

```
0:000> .symfix c:\mss
```

Then we put a breakpoint to main function and run the program until WinDbg breaks in:

```
0:000> bp main
```

```
0:000> g
Breakpoint 0 hit
eax=003330c0 ebx=7ffd7000 ecx=00000001 edx=00333138 esi=7c9118f1
edi=00011970
eip=0042d600 esp=0012ff70 ebp=0012ffb8 iopl=0        nv up ei pl zr na pe nc
cs=001b  ss=0023  ds=0023  es=0023  fs=003b  gs=0000              efl=00000246
LocalVariables!main:
0042d600 55                 push    ebp
```

Next we disassemble our main function:

```
0:000> .asm no_code_bytes
Assembly options: no_code_bytes
```

```
0:000> uf main
LocalVariables!main [c:\wdpf\localvariables\localvariables.cpp @ 2]:
    2 0042d600 push     ebp
    2 0042d601 mov      ebp,esp
    2 0042d603 sub      esp,0D8h
    2 0042d609 push     ebx
    2 0042d60a push     esi
    2 0042d60b push     edi
    2 0042d60c lea      edi,[ebp-0D8h]
    2 0042d612 mov      ecx,36h
    2 0042d617 mov      eax,0CCCCCCCCh
    2 0042d61c rep stos dword ptr es:[edi]
    5 0042d61e mov      dword ptr [ebp-8],1
    6 0042d625 mov      dword ptr [ebp-14h],1
    8 0042d62c mov      eax,dword ptr [ebp-14h]
    8 0042d62f add      eax,dword ptr [ebp-8]
    8 0042d632 mov      dword ptr [ebp-14h],eax
    9 0042d635 mov      eax,dword ptr [ebp-8]
    9 0042d638 add      eax,1
    9 0042d63b mov      dword ptr [ebp-8],eax
   10 0042d63e mov      eax,dword ptr [ebp-8]
```

```
10 0042d641 imul    eax,dword ptr [ebp-14h]
10 0042d645 mov     dword ptr [ebp-14h],eax
12 0042d648 xor     eax,eax
13 0042d64a pop     edi
13 0042d64b pop     esi
13 0042d64c pop     ebx
13 0042d64d mov     esp,ebp
13 0042d64f pop     ebp
13 0042d650 ret
```

Its source code is the following:

```
int main(int argc, char* argv[])
{
        int a, b;
        a = 1;
        b = 1;
        b = b + a;
        ++a;
        b = a * b;
        return 0;
}
```

Below is the same assembly language code but with comments show-ing operations in pseudo-code and highlighting function prolog and epilog:

```
LocalVariables!main:
push    ebp                     ; establishing stack frame
mov     ebp,esp                 ;
sub     esp,0xd8                ; creating stack frame for locals
push    ebx                     ; saving registers that might be used
push    esi                     ;    outside
push    edi                     ;
lea     edi,[ebp-0xd8]          ; getting the lowest address of stack frame
mov     ecx,0x36                ; filling stack frame with 0xCC byte
mov     eax,0xcccccccc          ;
```

```
rep       stosd                      ;
mov       dword ptr [ebp-0x8],0x1     ; [a] = 1        ([ebp-0x8])
mov       dword ptr [ebp-0x14],0x1    ; [b] = 1        ([ebp-0x14])
mov       eax,[ebp-0x14]             ; eax := [b]
add       eax,[ebp-0x8]             ; eax := eax + [a]
mov       [ebp-0x14],eax            ; [b] := eax    (b = b + a)
mov       eax,[ebp-0x8]             ; eax := [a]
add       eax,0x1                  ; eax := eax + 1
mov       [ebp-0x8],eax            ; [a] := eax    (++a)
mov       eax,[ebp-0x8]             ; eax := [a]
imul      eax,[ebp-0x14]            ; eax := eax * [b]
mov       [ebp-0x14],eax            ; [b] := eax    (b = a * b)
xor       eax,eax                  ; eax := 0       (return value)
pop       edi                      ; restoring registers
pop       esi                      ;
pop       ebx                      ;
mov       esp,ebp                  ; restoring previous stack pointer
pop       ebp                      ; restoring previous stack frame
ret                                ; return 0
```

The following assembly language fragment is explained visually on Picture 10.5.

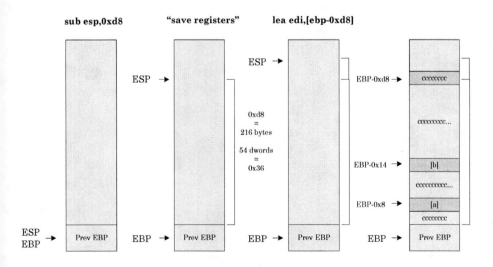

Picture 10.5

Disassembly of Optimized Executable (Release Configuration)

If we load LocalVariables.exe from Release project folder we would see very simple code that just returns 0:

```
0:000> uf main
LocalVariables!main [c:\wdpf\localvariables\localvariables.cpp @ 2]:
    2 00401000 xor      eax,eax
   13 00401002 ret
```

Where is all the code we have seen in Debug version? It was optimized away by Visual C++ compiler because the results of our calculation are never used. Variables a and b are local to main function and their values are not accessible outside when we return from the function.

Advanced Topic: FPO

FPO stands for Frame Pointer Omission; a kind of 32-bit code optimization where only ESP register is used to address local variables and parameters but EBP is used as a general purpose register like EAX.

Here is the same project assembly language code when compiled with FPO optimization enabled with comments showing operations in pseudo-code:

```
LocalVariables!main:
sub     esp,0x8          ; allocating stack space for locals
mov     eax,0x1          ; eax := 1
mov     [esp],eax        ; [a] := eax  ([esp])
mov     [esp+0x4],eax    ; [b] := eax  ([esp+0x4])
mov     eax,[esp+0x4]    ; eax := [b]
add     eax,[esp]        ; eax := eax + [a]
mov     [esp+0x4],eax    ; [b] := eax  (b = b + a)
mov     ecx,[esp]        ; ecx := [a]
inc     ecx              ; ecx += 1
mov     [esp],ecx        ; [a] := ecx  (++a)
mov     edx,[esp+0x4]    ; edx := [b]
mov     eax,[esp]        ; eax := [a]
imul    edx,eax          ; edx := edx * eax
mov     [esp+0x4],edx    ; [b] := edx  (b = b * a)
xor     eax,eax          ; eax := 0
add     esp,0x8          ; clearing stack space
ret                      ; return 0
```

Chapter 11: Function Parameters

"FunctionParameters" Project

In this chapter we learn how a caller function passes its parameters via stack memory and how a callee (the called function) accesses them. We will use the following project that can be downloaded from this ftp location:

ftp://dumpanalysis.org/pub/WDPF/Chapter11/

Here is the project source code:

```
// FunctionParameters.cpp
int arithmetic (int a, int b);
int main(int argc, char* argv[])
{
        int result = arithmetic (1, 1);
        return 0;
}
```

```
// Arithmetic.cpp
int arithmetic (int a, int b)
{
        b = b + a;
        ++a;
        b = a * b;
        return b;
}
```

Stack Structure

Recall from the previous chapter that EBP register is used to address stack memory locations. This was illustrated on Picture 10.1. Here we provide an example of the stack memory layout for the following function:

```
void func(int Param1, int Param2)
{
        int var1, var2;
        // stack memory layout at this point
        // ...
        // [EBP-8]      = var 1 (DWORD)
        // [EBP-4]      = var 1 (DWORD)
        // [EBP]        = previous EBP (DWORD)
        // [EBP+4]      = return address (DWORD)
        // [EBP+8]      = Param 1 (DWORD)
        // [EBP+C]      = Param 2 (DWORD)
        // ...
}
```

The stack frame memory layout for the function with 2 arguments and 2 local variables is illustrated on Picture 11.1.

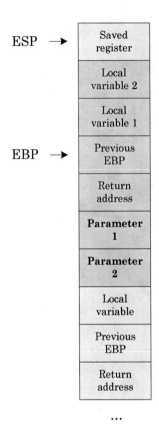

Picture 11.1

Stack Structure with FPO

With FPO introduced in the previous chapter we have the same stack memory layout but now ESP register is used to address stack memory double words:

```
void func(int Param1, int Param2)
{
        int var1, var2;
        // stack memory layout at this point
        // …
        // [ESP]        = var 2 (DWORD)
        // [ESP+4]      = var 1 (DWORD)
        // [ESP+8]      = return address (DWORD)
        // [ESP+C]      = Param 1 (DWORD)
        // [ESP+10]     = Param 2 (DWORD)
        // …
}
```

The stack frame memory layout for the function with 2 arguments and 2 local variables with FPO optimization enabled is illustrated on Picture 11.2.

ESP →

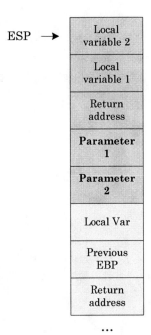

Picture 11.2

Function Prolog and Epilog

Now before we try to make sense of FunctionParameters project disassembly we look at the very simple case with one function parameter and one local variable to illustrate the standard function prolog and epilog sequence of instructions and corresponding stack memory changes.

Function prolog is illustrated on Picture 11.3 and function epilog is illustrated on Picture 11.4.

func() { func2(1); }   func2(int i) { int var; }

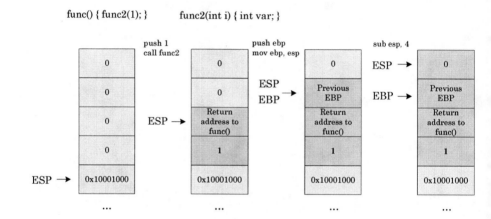

Picture 11.3

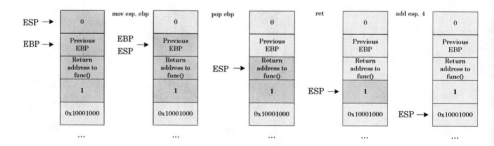

Picture 11.4

Project Disassembled Code with Comments

Here is commented code disassembly of main and arithmetic functions from Debug version of FunctionParameters.exe done by **uf** WinDbg command with memory addresses and codes removed for visual clarity.

```
FunctionParameters!main:
push    ebp                     ; establishing stack frame
mov     ebp,esp                 ;
sub     esp,0xcc                ; creating stack frame for local variables
push    ebx                     ; saving registers that might be used
push    esi                     ;    outside
push    edi                     ;
lea     edi,[ebp-0xcc]          ; getting the lowest address of stack frame
mov     ecx,0x33                ; filling stack frame with 0xCC
mov     eax,0xcccccccc          ;
rep     stosd                   ;
push    0x1                     ; push the rightmost parameter
push    0x1                     ; push next to the right parameter
call    FunctionParameters!ILT+845(?arithmeticYAHHHZ) (00411352)
add     esp,0x8                 ; adjusting stack (2 int parameters)
mov     [ebp-0x8],eax           ; save result to local variable
xor     eax,eax                 ; return value (0)
pop     edi                     ; restoring registers
pop     esi                     ;    (in reverse order)
pop     ebx                     ;
add     esp,0xcc                ; clearing stack
cmp     ebp,esp                 ; ESP == EBP ?
call    FunctionParameters!ILT+935(__RTC_CheckEsp) (004113ac)
mov     esp,ebp                 ; restoring previous stack pointer
pop     ebp                     ; restoring previous stack frame
ret                             ; return 0
```

```
FunctionParameters!arithmetic:

push    ebp                     ; establishing stack frame
mov     ebp,esp                 ;
sub     esp,0xc0                ; creating stack frame for locals
push    ebx                     ; saving registers that might be used
push    esi                     ;    outside
push    edi                     ;
lea     edi,[ebp-0xc0]          ; getting the lowest address of stack frame
mov     ecx,0x30                ; filling stack frame with 0xCC
mov     eax,0xcccccccc          ;
rep     stosd                   ;
mov     eax,[ebp+0xc]           ; eax := [b]
add     eax,[ebp+0x8]           ; eax += [a]
mov     [ebp+0xc],eax           ; [b] := eax    (b = b + a)
mov     eax,[ebp+0x8]           ; eax := [a]
add     eax,0x1                 ; eax := eax + 1
mov     [ebp+0x8],eax           ; [a] := eax    (++a)
mov     eax,[ebp+0x8]           ; eax := [a]
imul    eax,[ebp+0xc]           ; eax := eax * [b]
mov     [ebp+0xc],eax           ; [b] := eax    (b = a * b)
mov     eax,[ebp+0xc]           ; eax := [b]    (return value, b)
pop     edi                     ; restoring registers
pop     esi                     ;   (in reverse order)
pop     ebx                     ;
mov     esp,ebp                 ; restoring previous stack pointer
pop     ebp                     ; restoring previous stack frame
ret                             ; return 0
```

We can put a breakpoint on the first arithmetic calculations address and examine raw stack data pointed to by ESP register:

```
0:000> .asm no_code_bytes
Assembly options: no_code_bytes


0:000> uf arithmetic
FunctionParameters!arithmetic [c:\wdpf\functionparameters\arithmetic.cpp @
3]:
    3 0042d630 push    ebp
    3 0042d631 mov     ebp,esp
    3 0042d633 sub     esp,0C0h
    3 0042d639 push    ebx
    3 0042d63a push    esi
    3 0042d63b push    edi
    3 0042d63c lea     edi,[ebp-0C0h]
    3 0042d642 mov     ecx,30h
    3 0042d647 mov     eax,0CCCCCCCCh
    3 0042d64c rep stos dword ptr es:[edi]
    4 0042d64e mov     eax,dword ptr [ebp+0Ch]
    4 0042d651 add     eax,dword ptr [ebp+8]
    4 0042d654 mov     dword ptr [ebp+0Ch],eax
    5 0042d657 mov     eax,dword ptr [ebp+8]
    5 0042d65a add     eax,1
    5 0042d65d mov     dword ptr [ebp+8],eax
    6 0042d660 mov     eax,dword ptr [ebp+8]
    6 0042d663 imul    eax,dword ptr [ebp+0Ch]
    6 0042d667 mov     dword ptr [ebp+0Ch],eax
    8 0042d66a mov     eax,dword ptr [ebp+0Ch]
    9 0042d66d pop     edi
    9 0042d66e pop     esi
    9 0042d66f pop     ebx
    9 0042d670 mov     esp,ebp
    9 0042d672 pop     ebp
    9 0042d673 ret


0:000> bp 0042d64e
```

```
0:000> g

Breakpoint 1 hit
eax=cccccccc ebx=7ffda000 ecx=00000000 edx=00333140 esi=00cef77c
edi=0012fe84
eip=0042d64e esp=0012fdb8 ebp=0012fe84 iopl=0        nv up ei pl nz na po nc
cs=001b  ss=0023  ds=0023  es=0023  fs=003b  gs=0000            efl=00000202
FunctionParameters!arithmetic+0x1e:
0042d64e mov     eax,dword ptr [ebp+0Ch]        ss:0023:0012fe90=00000001


0:000> dds esp 140
0012fdb8  0012ff6c  ; saved EDI
0012fdbc  00cef77c  ;        ESI
0012fdc0  7ffda000  ;        EBX
0012fdc4  cccccccc
0012fdc8  cccccccc
0012fdcc  cccccccc
0012fdd0  cccccccc
0012fdd4  cccccccc
0012fdd8  cccccccc
0012fddc  cccccccc
0012fde0  cccccccc
0012fde4  cccccccc
0012fde8  cccccccc
0012fdec  cccccccc
0012fdf0  cccccccc
0012fdf4  cccccccc
0012fdf8  cccccccc
0012fdfc  cccccccc
0012fe00  cccccccc
0012fe04  cccccccc
0012fe08  cccccccc
0012fe0c  cccccccc
0012fe10  cccccccc
0012fe14  cccccccc
0012fe18  cccccccc
0012fe1c  cccccccc
0012fe20  cccccccc
0012fe24  cccccccc
0012fe28  cccccccc
0012fe2c  cccccccc
```

```
0012fe30   cccccccc
0012fe34   cccccccc
0012fe38   cccccccc
0012fe3c   cccccccc
0012fe40   cccccccc
0012fe44   cccccccc
0012fe48   cccccccc
0012fe4c   cccccccc
0012fe50   cccccccc
0012fe54   cccccccc
0012fe58   cccccccc
0012fe5c   cccccccc
0012fe60   cccccccc
0012fe64   cccccccc
0012fe68   cccccccc
0012fe6c   cccccccc
0012fe70   cccccccc
0012fe74   cccccccc
0012fe78   cccccccc
0012fe7c   cccccccc
0012fe80   cccccccc
0012fe84   0012ff6c   ; previous EBP
0012fe88   0042d6b7 FunctionParameters!main+0x27
[c:\wdpf\functionparameters\functionparameters.cpp @ 5] ; return address
0012fe8c   00000001   ; parameter 1
0012fe90   00000001   ; parameter 2
0012fe94   00cef6f2
0012fe98   00cef77c
0012fe9c   7ffda000
0012fea0   cccccccc
0012fea4   cccccccc
0012fea8   cccccccc
0012feac   cccccccc
0012feb0   cccccccc
0012feb4   cccccccc
```

Release Build with FPO Enabled

Release version of FunctionParameters.exe was compiled with FPO enabled and here is the corresponding code disassembly with comments:

FunctionParameters!main:

```
push    0x1                 ; parameter 2
push    0x1                 ; parameter 1
call    FunctionParameters!arithmetic (00401010)
add     esp, 0x8            ; adjusting stack
xor     eax, eax            ; return result 0
ret
```

FunctionParameters!arithmetic:

```
mov     eax, [esp+0x4]      ; eax := [b]
mov     ecx, [esp+0x8]      ; ecx := [a]
add     ecx, eax            ; ecx := ecx + eax
inc     eax                 ; eax := eax + 1
imul    eax, ecx            ; eax := eax * ecx
ret                         ; return result in eax
```

Cdecl Calling Convention

When looking at pictures and commented assembly language code we have seen that function parameters are passed from right to left and the caller is responsible for adjusting the stack after calling the callee function. This is the so called **cdecl** calling convention in C and C++. It allows calling functions with variable number of parameters, for example, printf and scanf:

```
printf("result = %d", nVal);
```

Here is the corresponding stack memory layout:

```
EBP -> Previous EBP
       Return address
       The address of "" string
       The value of nVal variable
```

Another C code example and the following corresponding stack memory layout:

```
printf("left: %d right: %d top: %d bottom: %d", nLeft, nRight, nTop,
       nBottom);


EBP -> Previous EBP
       Return address
       The address of "" string
       The value of nLeft variable
       The value of nRight variable
       The value of nTop variable
       The value of nBottom variable
```

Parameter Mismatch Problem

To illustrate the importance of understanding stack memory layout consider this typical interface mismatch problem. Function main calls func with two parameters:

```
// main.c
int main ()
{
        int locVar;
        func (1, 2);
        return 0;
}
```

The caller is expected the callee function func to see this stack memory layout:

```
EBP -> Previous EBP
       Return address
       1
       2
       locVar
```

However the caller expects 3 parameters instead of 2:

```
// func.c
int func (int a, int b, int c)
{
    // code to use parameters
    return 0;
}
```

Func code sees this stack memory layout:

```
EBP -> Previous EBP
       Return address
       a
       b
       c
```

We see that parameter c coincides with locVar local main function variable and this is clearly a software defect (bug).

Chapter 12: More Instructions

CPU Flags Register

In addition to registers CPU also contains a special 32–bit EFLAGS register where certain bits are set or cleared in response to arithmetic and other operations. Some bit values can be manipulated by separate machine instructions and their value affects code execution.

For example, DF bit (Direction Flag) determines the direction of memory copy operations and can be set by STD and cleared by CLD instructions. It has the default value of 0 and its location is shown on Picture 12.1.

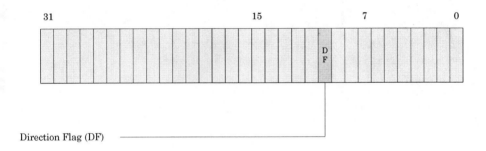

Picture 12.

The Fastest Way to Fill Memory

This is done by STOSD instruction that stores a dword value from EAX into a memory location which address is in EDI register ("D" means destination). After the value from EAX is transferred to memory the instruction increments EDI by 4 and EDI register now points to the next DWORD in memory if DF flag is 0. If DF flag is 1 then EDI value is decremented by 4 and EDI now points to the previous DWORD in memory.

If we prefix any instruction with REP prefix it causes the instruction to be repeated until the value in ECX register is decremented to 0. For example we can write very simple code that should theoretically zero "all memory" (practically it will trap because of access violation):

```
xor eax, eax           ; fill with 0
mov edi, 0             ; starting address or xor edi, edi
mov ecx, 0xffffffff / 4    ; 0x3fffffff dwords
rep stosd
```

Here is REP STOSD in pseudo-code:

```
WHILE (ECX != 0)
{
      [EDI] := EAX

      IF DF = 0 THEN
            EDI := EDI + 4
      ELSE
            EDI := EDI - 4

      ECX := ECX - 1
}
```

Simple example of erasing 16 bytes (4x4) is shown on Picture 12.2.

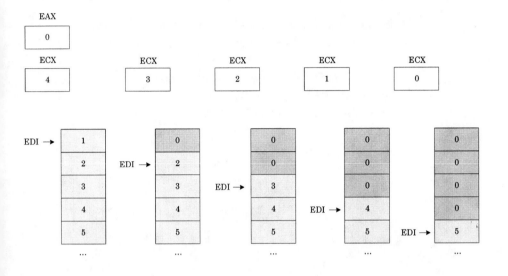

Picture 12.2

Testing for 0

ZF bit in EFLAGS register is set to 1 if the instruction result is 0 and cleared otherwise. This bit is affected by:

- Arithmetic instructions (for example, ADD, SUB, MUL)
- Logical compare instruction (TEST)
- "Arithmetical" compare instruction (CMP)

The location of ZF bit is shown on Picture 12.3.

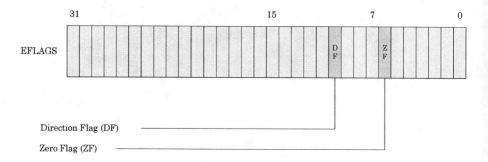

Picture 12.3

TEST - Logical Compare

This instruction computes bit-wise logical AND between both operands and sets flags (including ZF) according to the computed result (which is discarded):

```
TEST reg/mem, reg/imm
```

Examples:

```
TEST EDX, EDX
```

Suppose EDX register contains 4 (100_{bin})

100_{bin} AND 100_{bin} = 100_{bin} != 0 (ZF is cleared)

```
TEST EDX, 1
```

Suppose EDX contains 0 (0_{bin})

0_{bin} AND 1_{bin} = 0_{bin} == 0 (ZF is set)

Here is TEST instruction in pseudo-code (details not relevant to ZF bit are omitted):

```
TEMP := OPERAND1 AND OPERAND2
IF TEMP = 0 THEN
        ZF := 1
ELSE
        ZF := 0
```

CMP – Compare Two Operands

This instruction compares the first operand with the second and sets flags (including ZF) according to the computed result (which is discarded). Comparison is performed by subtracting the second operand from the first (like SUB instruction: SUB EAX, 4).

```
CMP reg/mem, reg/imm

CMP reg, reg/mem/imm
```

Examples:

```
CMP EDI, 0
```

Suppose EDI contains 0

$0 - 0 == 0$ (ZF is set)

```
CMP EAX, 16
```

Suppose EAX contains 4_{hex}

$4_{hex} - 16_{hex} = FFFFFFEE_{hex}$!= 0 (ZF is cleared)

$4_{dec} - 22_{dec} = -18_{dec}$

Here is CMP instruction in pseudo-code (details not relevant to ZF bit are omitted):

```
TEMP := OPERAND1 - OPERAND2
IF TEMP = 0 THEN
      ZF := 1
ELSE
      ZF := 0
```

CMP instruction is equivalent to this pseudo-code sequence:

```
TEMP := OPERAND1
SUB TEMP, OPERAND2
```

TEST or CMP?

They are equivalent if we want to test for zero, but CMP instruction affects more flags:

```
TEST EAX, EAX

CMP  EAX, 0
```

CMP instruction is used to compare for inequality (TEST instruction cannot be used here):

```
CMP EAX, 0          ; > 0 or < 0 ?
```

TEST instruction is used to see if individual bit is set

```
TEST EAX, 2  ; 2 == 0010bin or in C language: if (var & 0x2)
```

Examples where EAX has the value of 2:

```
TEST EAX, 4   ; 0010bin AND 0100bin = 0000bin (ZF is set)

TEST EAX, 6   ; 0010bin AND 0110bin = 0010bin (ZF is cleared)
```

Conditional Jumps

Consider these two C or C++ code fragments:

```
if (a == 0)                          if (a != 0)
{                                    {
    ++a;                                 ++a;
}                                    }
else                                 else
{                                    {
    --a;                                 --a;
}                                    }
```

CPU fetches instructions sequentially, so we must tell CPU that we want to skip some instructions if some condition is (not) met, for example, if a != 0.

JNZ (jump if not zero) and JZ (jump if zero) test ZF flag and change EIP if ZF bit is cleared for JZN or set for JZ. The following assembly language code is equivalent to C/C++ code above:

```
        CMP   [A], 0                    MOV   EAX, [A]
        JNZ   label1                    TEST  EAX, EAX
        INC   [A]                       JZ    label1
        JMP   label2                    INC   EAX
label1: DEC      [A]                    JMP   label2
label2:                         label1: DEC   EAX
                                label2:
```

The Structure of Registers

32-bit register have 16-bit legacy structure that allows us to address their lower 16-bit and two 8-bit parts as shown on Picture 12.4.

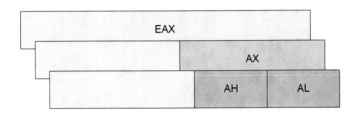

Picture 12.4

Never read a book about Intel assembly language that uses AX, BX and other 16-bit legacy in examples throughout the text.

I remember 10 years ago I met a guy who was interviewed for a job at Intel. They asked him about assembly language. The guy started talking about AX and BX. No wonder he wasn't hired. This is probably similar to being enthusiastic about Java and Solaris during Microsoft job interview.

Function Return Value

Many functions return values via EAX register. For example:

```
int func();
```

return value is in EAX

```
bool func();
```

return value is in AL

Note: bool values occupy one byte in memory.

Using Byte Registers

Suppose we have a byte value in AL register and we want to add this value to ECX register. However we don't know what values other parts of full EAX register contain. We cannot use this instruction:

```
MOV    EBX, AL    ; operand size conflict
```

The proposed solution in pseudo-code:

```
EBX := AL           or      EAX := AL

ECX := ECX + EBX            ECX := ECX + EAX
```

We can only use MOV instructions that have the same operand size for both source and destination, for example:

```
MOV    BL, AL

MOV    byte ptr [b], AL   ; in C: static bool b = func()
```

For this task there is a special MOVZX (Move with Zero eXtend) instruction that replaces the contents of the first operand with the contents of the second operand while filling the rest of bits with zeros:

```
MOVZX reg, reg/mem
```

Therefore our solution for the task becomes very simple:

```
MOVZX EBX, AL
ADD    ECX, EBX
```

We can also reuse EAX register:

```
MOVZX EAX, AL
ADD    ECX, EAX
```

Chapter 13: Function Pointer Parameters

"FunctionPointerParameters" Project

This is our final project and it can be downloaded from

ftp://dumpanalysis.org/pub/WDPF/Chapter13/

The project source code:

```cpp
// FunctionParameters.cpp
int main(int argc, char* argv[])
{
        int a, b;

        printf("Enter a and b: ");
        scanf("%d %d", &a, &b);

        if (arithmetic (a, &b))
        {
                printf("Result = %d", b);
        }

        return 0;
}


// Arithmetic.cpp
bool arithmetic (int a, int *b)
{
        if (!b)
        {
                return false;
        }

        *b = *b + a;
        ++a;
        *b = a * *b;

        return true;
}
```

Commented Disassembly

Here is the commented disassembly from Debug executable. FPO optimization was disabled.

```
FunctionParameters!main:
push    ebp                 ; establishing stack frame
mov     ebp,esp             ;
sub     esp,0xd8            ; creating stack frame for locals
push    ebx                 ; saving registers that might be used
push    esi                 ;    outside
push    edi                 ;
lea     edi,[ebp-0xd8]      ; getting the lowest address of stack frame
mov     ecx,0x36            ; filling stack frame with 0xCC
mov     eax,0xcccccccc      ;
rep     stosd               ;
push    0x427034            ; address of "Enter a and b: " string
call    FunctionParameters!ILT+1285(_printf) (0041150a)
add     esp,0x4             ; adjust stack pointer (1 parameter)
lea     eax,[ebp-0x14]      ; address of b
push    eax                 ;
lea     ecx,[ebp-0x8]       ; address of a
push    ecx                 ;
push    0x42702c            ; address of "%d %d" string
call    FunctionParameters!ILT+990(_scanf) (004113e3)
add     esp,0xc             ; adjust stack pointer (3 parameters,
                            ;   3*4 = 12 bytes, 0xc in hexadecimal)
lea     eax,[ebp-0x14]      ; address of b
push    eax                 ;
mov     ecx,[ebp-0x8]       ; value of a
push    ecx                 ;
call    FunctionParameters!ILT+535(?arithmeticYA_NHPAHZ) (0041121c)
add     esp,0x8             ; adjust stack pointer (2 parameters)
movzx   edx,al              ; bool result from arithmetic
test    edx,edx             ; testing for zero
jz      FunctionParameters!main+0x68 (00411bf8)
mov     eax,[ebp-0x14]      ; value of b
push    eax                 ;
push    0x42701c            ; address of "Result = %d" string
```

```
call      FunctionParameters!ILT+1285(_printf) (0041150a)
add       esp,0x8                 ; adjust stack pointer (2 variables)
00411bf8:
xor       eax,eax                 ; return result 0
push      edx                     ; saving register ?
mov       ecx,ebp                 ; passing parameter via ecx
push      eax                     ; saving register ?
lea       edx,[FunctionParameters!main+0x8f (00411c1f)] ; probably address
                                  ;           of information about stack frame
call      FunctionParameters!ILT+455(_RTC_CheckStackVars (004111cc)
pop       eax                     ; restoring registers
pop       edx                     ;
pop       edi                     ;
pop       esi                     ;
pop       ebx                     ;
add       esp,0xd8                ; adjusting stack pointer
cmp       ebp,esp                 ; ESP == EBP ?
call      FunctionParameters!ILT+1035(__RTC_CheckEsp) (00411410)
mov       esp,ebp                 ; restoring previous stack pointer
pop       ebp                     ; restoring previous stack frame
ret                               ; return
```

```
FunctionParameters!arithmetic:

push    ebp

mov     ebp,esp

sub     esp,0xc0

push    ebx

push    esi

push    edi

lea     edi,[ebp-0xc0]

mov     ecx,0x30

mov     eax,0xcccccccc

rep     stosd

cmp     dword ptr [ebp+0xc],0x0      ; &b == 0 ?

jnz     FunctionParameters!arithmetic+0x28 (00411b48)

xor     al,al                       ; return bool value false (0)

jmp     FunctionParameters!arithmetic+0x4e (00411b6e)

00411b48:

mov     eax,[ebp+0xc]               ; eax := address of b

mov     ecx,[eax]

add     ecx,[ebp+0x8]               ; ecx := ecx + [a]     (in C: t = *b + a)

mov     edx,[ebp+0xc]               ; edx := address of b

mov     [edx],ecx                   ;                      (in C: *b := t)

mov     eax,[ebp+0x8]               ; eax := [a]    (in C: ++a)

add     eax,0x1

mov     [ebp+0x8],eax               ; [a] := eax

mov     eax,[ebp+0xc]               ; eax := address of b

mov     ecx,[ebp+0x8]               ; ecx := [a]

imul    ecx,[eax]                   ; ecx := ecx * [b]   (in C: t = a * *b)

mov     edx,[ebp+0xc]               ; edx := address of b

mov     [edx],ecx                   ;                      (in C: *b = t)

mov     al,0x1                      ; return bool value true (0)

00411b6e:

pop     edi

pop     esi

pop     ebx

mov     esp,ebp

pop     ebp

ret
```

Dynamic Addressing of Local Variables

Here is the commented disassembly from Release executable. FPO optimization was enabled and this provides an excellent example of dynamic variable addressing via ESP register.

```
FunctionParameters!main:

sub      esp,0x8                  ; allocating room for local variables

push     0x408110                 ; address of "Enter a and b: "

call     FunctionParameters!printf (00401085)

lea      eax,[esp+0x4]            ; address of b    ([ESP + 0 + 4])

push     eax

lea      ecx,[esp+0xc]            ; address of a    ([ESP + 4 + 8])

push     ecx

push     0x408108                 ; address of "%d %d"

call     FunctionParameters!scanf (0040106e)

mov      eax,[esp+0x14]           ; value of a      ([ESP + 4 + 10])

lea      edx,[esp+0x10]           ; address of b    ([ESP + 0 + 10])

push     edx

push     eax

call     FunctionParameters!arithmetic (00401000)

add      esp,0x18                 ; adjusting stack after all pushes

test     al,al                    ; al == 0 ?

jz       FunctionParameters!main+0x48 (00401068)

mov      ecx,[esp]                ; address of b    ([ESP + 0])

push     ecx

push     0x4080fc                 ; address of "Result = %d"

call     FunctionParameters!printf (00401085)

add      esp,0x8                  ; adjust stack pointer (2 parameters)

00401068:

xor      eax,eax                  ; return value 0

add      esp,0x8                  ; adjust stack pointer (local variables)

ret
```

```
FunctionParameters!arithmetic:
mov      eax,[esp+0x8]           ; address of b
test     eax,eax                 ; &b == 0 ?
jnz      FunctionParameters!arithmetic+0xb (0040100b)
xor      al,al                   ; return value false (0)
ret
0040100b:
mov      edx,[eax]               ; edx := [b]   (in C: *b)
mov      ecx,[esp+0x4]           ; ecx := [a]
add      edx,ecx
inc      ecx
imul     edx,ecx
mov      [eax],edx               ; [b] := edx
mov      al,0x1                  ; return value true (1)
ret
```

Chapter 14: Summary of Code Disassembly Patterns

This final chapter summarizes various patterns we have encountered during the reading of this book.

Function Prolog / Epilog

Function prolog

```
push    ebp
mov     ebp,esp
```

Function epilog

```
mov     esp,ebp
pop     ebp
ret     [number]
```

In some old legacy code this is equivalent to:

```
leave
ret     [number]
```

Knowing prolog can help in identifying situations when symbol files or function start addresses are not correct. For example, suppose you have the following stack trace:

```
func3+0x5F
func2+0x8F
func+0x20
```

If we disassemble func2 function and see that it doesn't start with prolog we may assume that stack trace needs more attention:

```
0:000> u func2 func2+0x8F
add   ecx, 10
mov   eax, [ebx+10]
push ebp
mov   ebp, esp
...
```

Passing Parameters

Local variable address

```
[ebp - XXX]
```

Function parameter address

```
[ebp + XXX]
```

Useful mnemonic: first push parameters (+, up) then use local variables (-, down).

Static/global variable address (or string constant)

```
push    0x427034
```

Local variable vs. local variable address

```
mov     reg, [ebp-XXX]
push    reg                     ; local variable
...
call    func


lea     reg, [ebp-XXX]
push    reg                     ; local variable address
...
call    func
```

LEA (Load Effective Address)

The following instruction

```
lea    eax, [ebp-0x8]
```

is equivalent to the following arithmetic sequence:

```
mov    eax, ebp
sub    eax, 0x8
```

Accessing Parameters and Local Variables

Accessing DWORD parameter

```
mov      eax, [ebp+0x8]
add      eax, 0x1
```

Accessing a pointer to a DWORD value

```
lea      eax, [ebp+0x8]
mov      eax, [eax]
add      eax, 0x1
```

Accessing a local DWORD value

```
mov      eax, [ebp-0x8]
add      eax, 0x1
```

Accessing a pointer to a DWORD local variable

```
lea      eax, [ebp-0x8]
mov      eax, [eax]
add      eax, 0x1
```

OpenTask books

#1 Debugging Bestseller on Amazon

Memory Dump Analysis Anthology, Volume 1

Author: Dmitry Vostokov

ISBN-13: 978-0-9558328-0-2 (Paperback, 720 pages)

ISBN-13: 978-0-9558328-1-9 (Hardcover, 720 pages)

This is a revised, edited, cross-referenced and thematically organized volume of selected DumpAnalysis.org blog posts about crash dump analysis and debugging written in 2006 - 2007 for software engineers developing and maintaining products on Windows platforms, quality assurance engineers testing software on Windows platforms, technical support and escalation engineers dealing with complex software issues and general Windows users.

The back cover image is the picture of TestDefaultDebugger crash dump generated by Dump2Picture.

Memory Dump Analysis Anthology, Volume 2

Author: Dmitry Vostokov

ISBN-13: 978-0-9558328-7-1 (Paperback, 470 pages)

ISBN-13: 978-1-906717-22-3 (Hardcover, 470 pages)

This is a revised, edited, cross-referenced and thematically organized volume of selected DumpAnalysis.org blog posts about crash dump analysis and debugging written in January - September 2008 for software engineers developing and maintaining products on Windows platforms, quality assurance engineers testing software on Windows platforms and technical support and escalation engineers dealing with complex software issues. The second volume features:

- 45 new crash dump analysis patterns
- Pattern interaction and case studies
- Updated checklist
- Fully cross-referenced with Volume 1
- New appendixes

Back cover features visualized virtual process memory generated from a memory dump of colometric computer memory dating sample using Dump2Picture.

WinDbg: A Reference Poster and Learning Cards

Author: Dmitry Vostokov

ISBN-13: 978-1-906717-29-2 (Full color paperback, 20 pages)

WinDbg is a powerful debugger from Microsoft Debugging Tools for Windows. It has more than 350 commands that can be used in different debugging scenarios. The cover of this book is a poster featuring crash dump analysis checklist and common patterns seen in memory dumps and live debugging sessions. Inside the book you can find ready to cut learning cards with commands and their descriptions colored according to their use for crash dump or live debugging sessions and user, kernel or complete memory dumps. Tossing cards can create unexpected connections between commands and help to learn them more quickly. Uncut pages can also serve as birds eye view to WinDbg debugging capabilities. More than 350 WinDbg commands including meta-commands and extensions are included.

Dumps, Bugs and Debugging Forensics:
The Adventures of Dr. Debugalov

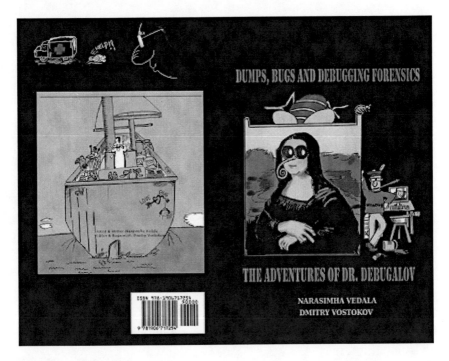

Author: Narasimha Vedala

Editor: Dmitry Vostokov

ISBN-13: 978-1-906717-25-4 (Full color paperback, 64 pages)

Finally Dr. Debugalov adventures are imprinted with bugs inside. The full-color book also features never published before cartoons and a few surprises. It sets a new standard for entertainment in software engineering.

DLL List Landscape:
The Art from Computer Memory Space

Author: Dmitry Vostokov

ISBN-13: 978-1-906717-36-0 (Full color paperback, 16 pages)

DLL is also a recursive acronym for **DLL List Landscape**. This new full color book features magnificent images from process user space generated by Dump2Picture.

The perfect binary gift

Baby Turing

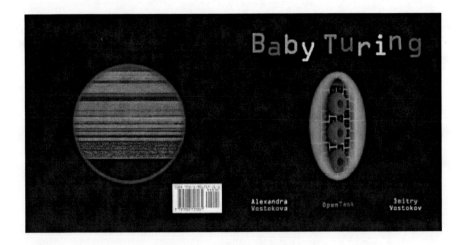

Authors: Alexandra Vostokova, Dmitry Vostokov

ISBN-13: 978-1-906717-26-1 (Full color paperback, 16 pages)

The genius of Albert Einstein was revolutionary in understanding reality of hardware (semantics of nature) but the genius of Alan Turing was revolutionary in understanding virtuality of software (syntax of computation). This book fills the gap in children's literature and introduces binary arithmetic to babies.

Printed in the United States
152041LV00001B/172/P